EDEN: Golden Age or Goad to Action?

ORBIS BOOKS
MARYKNOLL, NEW YORK

EDEN
Golden Age or Goad to Action?

Carlos Mesters

Translated by Patrick J. Leonard, C.S.Sp.

Originally published as *Paraıso terrestre: saudade ou esperanca*
by Editôra Vozes Ltda., Petropolis, Brazil, 1971
Copyright © 1974 Orbis Books, Maryknoll, New York 10545
Library of Congress Catalog Card Number: 74-78453
ISBN: 0-88344-103-9
Manufactured in the United States of America

Contents

Foreword

This little book is no more than an entrance way. For many people the Old Testament is a sort of maze. They cannot tell which doorway will lead them inside. There are good books that tell about the entrance and how it may be found. But instead of speaking about the entrance, we prefer to take the reader right inside this strange world of the Bible. It remains a strange world for the one who comes in by the wrong door. But the one who comes in the correct way hardly notices that he is in another world; rather he feels that he is still in the world he knows. Let this be our reader's way of judging whether this little book is really the right entrance.

We use hardly any quotes. Only at the end is there a bibliography. This is no accident. For a long time before starting to write this book, before it was even thought of, we had been reading widely around the theme. Little by little, as life unfolded, a synthesis was also unfolding. Rather than books, faith and life's problems were our guide. And life is something known and lived, not something you can reduce to quotes. However, anyone who finds it hard to accept our arguments can always consult the sources covered by the bibliography.

The name of Professor Jean Audet does not occur in the bibliography. As far as we know he has not written on this theme. Yet to his courses about Paradise given in Jerusalem, we owe many of the thoughts of this book. Without his lead, it would never have seen the light. So in a sense it is his progeny too.

Introduction

World literature is full of commentaries on the earthly paradise. There are no fewer than two hundred interpretations of the serpent narrative alone (Gen. 3:1). So any interpretation, whether the one we learned in the past or the one given in this book, is of necessity relative. Interpretations have the very limited but very important task of keeping free a way for the Word of God, so that the Word may be effective in the lives and the history of men. But it is the Word that remains central, not the ideas of the exegete. It is the Word that must reach the conscience of men in all its purity, with all that it demands and promises, so as to bring about a conversion of life and a transformation of reality.

Outlook and culture are constantly changing. So too the way we regard and interpret the Bible. We are running into a lot of problems today with the Paradise narrative precisely because we have not changed our interpretation, because our exegesis has not changed our interpretation, because our exegesis has not kept up with the changes in our lives. Many find it impossible today to understand the exact meaning of the biblical narrative on Paradise and the sin of Adam and Eve.

The problem is like a highway closed to traffic. Cars are detoured through narrow streets and at times become lost in dead ends. God's message, coming to us by the highway of the Bible, is diverted into the narrow streets and is no longer recognizable. It cannot reach its final destination—the transformation of the life and history of men.

We want to speak of Paradise and the sin of Adam and Eve in a way that will guide the reader through this maze and finally get him back on the wide road of God's transforming Word. We will begin by surveying the difficulties that lead us into side roads and into dead ends and keep us from seeing what the text really means. The reader may recognize some of his problems or be able to pinpoint the doubts he experiences when he reads this part of the Bible.

Then comes the interpretation of the biblical text. Our aim will be to bring out—within the context of our daily life—the call and the message of God hidden there. This call and this message await the one who discovers them, accepts them, and puts them into practice.

Next we will come back to the difficulties. In the light of our interpretation we will try to guide the reader along an escape route from the maze so that he may find again the open highway of the Word of God and reach his destination.

Then, we offer a new translation of the biblical text, direct from the Hebrew. It tries to be faithful not only to the original but also to our language and culture. We hope that by constantly referring to it the reader may more easily follow our presentation (see pp. 83–107).

Finally, we consider the doctrine of original sin.

EDEN: Golden Age or Goad to Action?

CHAPTER ONE

Difficulties Concerning Paradise and Adam's Sin

Not all the difficulties we might think of are equally important. Some are real, others imaginary. But all are serious for the one who experiences them, and so we must treat them seriously, analyze, criticize and respond to them.

Some arise directly from the biblical text. Others come from the challenges of science or from conflict with the findings of modern exegesis or statements of the magisterium of the Church. We will list them insofar as we can and evaluate them to see if we can find their common root cause.

Questions Raised by the Text Itself

How could a man be formed from the dust of the earth (Gen. 2:7)? Is it true that the woman was made from the rib of the man (Gen. 2:21–22)? Were the first two humans really called Adam and Eve? How can the Bible speak of God in the role of potter (Gen. 2:7) and anesthetist (Gen. 2:21)? Or what should we think of a talking snake (Gen. 3:1–4)? Animals do not speak: Is this just a fable or should we say that the animals in Paradise really spoke? Did snakes have another kind of locomotion before the sin of Adam (Gen. 3:14)? If Eve had not eaten that fruit, would we now have painless childbirth (Gen. 3:16)? Would there be no deserts if Adam had not listened to his wife (Gen. 3:17)? Would we all be going around naked if our first parents had not committed that sin (Gen. 3:7)? Why do we identify the serpent with Satan when the Bible does not make this identification in the narrative?

The Bible speaks of a river which, after irrigating Paradise, divides into four different branches: the Nile, the Ganges, the Tigris, and the Euphrates (Gen. 2:10–14). Was there really a single geographic point where these four rivers could have arisen? Our geography does not recognize any such point and nothing indicates any major change in the earth since then. The Bible seems to be speaking of an imaginary place, but how can we reconcile this with our traditional idea of the earthly paradise?

How could God make the ruin of everyone depend on the sin of one couple? Was he unjust? Why do we today have to suffer the consequences of a sin we did not commit, against which we could not react, and of which we have neither consciousness nor memory?

In Gen. 1:26–27 man is the last to be created. In Gen. 2:7 he is the first. How do we explain this contradiction in the Bible within the space of a few pages?

The Bible tells us that God did not destroy Paradise. It continued to exist after the sin of Adam and Eve (Gen. 3:23–24). But God put cherubim and a sword there to guard the entrance to the tree of life against man. Was God so afraid of man? Who exactly are the cherubim? Can we even imagine a sword guarding the entrance to an orchard? Do the remains of this lost Paradise still exist today somewhere on earth? Some speak of undertaking an expedition to find it; will it be found some day, thus confirming the words of the Bible?

We all have these and other difficulties from time to time —some quietly, others loudly. Some think that even to ask such questions is a sin; others are not so concerned and freely question and criticize.

Science Questions the Bible

In the conflict between science and faith or, on a more popular level, between common sense and catechism, the story of Adam and Eve is a major bone of contention.

Science today supports the theory of evolution, while the Bible describes the creation of man and woman as a direct act (Gen. 2:7,

21–22). These positions are mutually exclusive. Which is correct? If science is right, how do we explain the biblical text?

Moreover, it is hard to reconcile the traditional concept of original sin with the theory of evolution. A man and a woman, even before they had children, committed a fault so serious that they compromised forever the destiny of all their descendants. Thus they lost the so-called *supernatural* and *preternatural* gifts which faith and theology attribute to them. Science indicates the utter improbability of this. Primitive man could not have had a consciousness, freedom, maturity, and sense of responsibility sufficiently evolved and perfected to be capable of committing such a serious fault nor could have possessed such sublime gifts. All available scientific evidence regarding primitive man indicates exactly the opposite.

There is always the real possibility that one day we may have to admit polygenesis—the theory that mankind did not originate with just one couple but rather with several couples in various parts of the globe. Science still does not have sufficient proof to confirm this hypothesis and many scientists do not hold it. But if it were to be proved some day, would it still be possible to hold that a single sin committed by a single couple contaminated the whole of mankind at the dawn of history?

Therefore, although it does not offer absolute certainty in its conclusions, science today radically questions the whole set of beliefs based on the traditional explanation of Paradise.

The Church, no doubt, could use its authority to prohibit such scientific conclusions. Yet this would not disprove the conclusions, since science is not based on theology but on its own autonomous principles of investigation. Such a Church prohibition would backfire. Some Christians would stop studying the findings of science and so end up without any real argument to defend their faith against its objections.

The result would be—as it has been for many—the total rejection of a faith that fears to confront the truth and has no answers for the questions of science. An even worse result is the suppressed conflict of those who are well informed regarding the findings of science. Notwithstanding their openness to science, they maintain a traditional position regarding faith and the Bible which often contradicts the scientific conclusions they have accepted. They do not see the contradiction and even refuse to discuss the subject.

This theoretical conflict between science and faith leads in practice to a complete separation between intelligence and religion. Their position of seeming fidelity to authority and tradition is in fact further from the truth than that of those who reject the faith in the name of science or science in the name of faith.

Modern Exegesis Challenges Accepted Beliefs

What were the sources of information of the writer of the Paradise narrative? Many do not even ask this question. For them, if something is in the Bible there is no questioning. These people forget that this divine book was written by men, in a very human way, using the same literary methods and processes that go into the writing of any other book. We know now that the literature of antiquity had many similar narratives which could have served as source material for the biblical author. We know too how the source can condition what is transmitted. So why should we be surprised at the question, "Where did the writer of the the Bible get his information about Paradise and the sin of Adam and Eve?" The question can and must be asked since nothing that is human, except deliberate lying, is foreign to the Bible.

There are two traditional explanations: Either the story originated in an oral tradition, handed down without interruption from the first people, or else the author learned everything from a direct divine revelation. The real problem posed by these answers is that each would require a miracle, and we are not justified in resorting to a miracle when there is a natural explanation. Why do we say that each requires a miracle?

Humanly speaking we cannot accept the idea of an uninterrupted oral tradition covering a million years or more. Only a miracle would explain the survival of such a tradition. Even with the help of better means of communication we can have only a faint idea of what happened on the day that America was discovered —and this was less than 500 years ago. How could we have such a detailed account passed on by word of mouth of something that happened hundreds of thousands of years earlier? The Bible itself gives no indication of such an uninterrupted miraculous tradition. Its only basis is our inability to give a more satisfactory explanation of the origin of the text.

Can we accept the second hypothesis, that God himself revealed to the author all the details concerning creation and what happened to the first man? This hypothesis has no foundation at all, except that it fulfills a psychological need for certainty and security; in the Bible, God is not in the habit of revealing to man the details of his actions, future or past. He reveals only certainties, stirring up hopes. For example, the prophets themselves, guided by the Spirit of God, imagined the details of their prophetic visions of the future on the basis of what they knew of past events.

There is a third possibility: The author composed the narrative using the images and symbols of his time, drawing on the common cultural heritage of the peoples of the Ancient Middle East. His description of Paradise would then have resulted from some human discovery. But how, then, would the Bible differ from the myths of antiquity? What would be the historical value of Paradise and the sin of Adam and Eve? In this case could the author give us a minute description of what really happened so long before? Humanly speaking, with our modern discoveries we are really in a much better position than he to describe objectively what took place at the dawn of history. Writing in the tenth century B.C., the biblical author was hundreds of times closer to our twentieth century than he was to the beginnings of mankind.

Difficulties Arising Today
from Decisions of Church Authority

In 1909 when debate about the earthly Paradise was at its height, the Pontifical Biblical Commission pronounced that the Catholic exegete must hold as historical, among other things, that woman was formed from the first man (Gen. 2:21–23); the unity of the human races, sprung from one couple (Gen. 3:20); the divine command to test the obedience of our first parents (Gen. 2:17); the Serpent that tempted Eve (Gen. 3:1–4); the fall from a previous state of perfection characterized by justice, integrity, and immortality.

But today we know of many other accounts from ancient times which tell of the Serpent, a previous state of happiness and immortality, the tree of life, etc. We have no difficulty in admitting that these are myths, that their language is symbolic and that their origin, meaning, and implications may be explained by the study of ancient religions.

Can we admit the same for the biblical narrative? Can biblical language be put on the same footing as the mythical language of the other peoples of that time? If so, what are we to say of the declaration of the Pontifical Biblical Commission? What of the historical value of the Paradise narrative? To what are we bound by a decree of 1909, when neither theology nor science had facts we now have? What of the papal encyclical *Humani generis* in which Pope Pius XII used the Catholic doctrine of original sin to forbid Catholics from holding the hypothesis of polygenism?

Three Different Ways of Facing the Difficulties

Such are the difficulties. The results of scientific research and the theories of theologians and exegetes are no longer the preserve of the intelligentsia, but are topics of everyday conversation.

All of this shows that without realizing it we are held captive by a predetermined way of seeing and interpreting earthly Paradise. This is the pattern created in our minds by the traditional teaching of the catechism. But science and common sense make us have serious reservations about our traditional approach and give us the feeling that something is wrong somewhere. We feel that somehow the foundations of our religious convictions are not as firm, do not give us the same security as before. Deep down many no longer believe what the Bible says in these pages, yet they do not know how to formulate or explain their doubts. They even fear them and try to hide behind the questions we listed above.

The reason for this vague feeling of uneasiness is probably that we so identify God's revelation with our traditional viewpoint that we cannot separate one from the other. Many indeed are convinced that to abandon the traditional approach is to abandon all revealed truth. This causes insecurity. In order not to deny their faith, they vainly take issue with science, with common sense, and with any approach to revelation other than the traditional one. In fact these people are defending their own viewpoint, their own cherished ideas, their own psychological security. They are defending a particular way of looking at revelation rather than defending revelation itself. They do not see the relativity of their position. They forget that there are thousands of interpretations of the Paradise narrative, claiming that their way of seeing things is the only way. And this is not done for love of truth, but for love of a sense of security they do not wish to lose. Naturally this security motive is a value and is not to be rejected out of hand or despised.

Others adopt the opposite attitude. They turn to science and reject the biblical narrative as childish and out of date. Both of these polarized positions stem from the same preconceived idea. Both groups of people have identified revelation with one of its many interpretations. Their reaction is not against revealed truth but rather against a certain way of explaining that truth.

The third position is the one we have already referred to. Its adherents admit everything that science says in its field but continue to hold everything taught about the traditional interpretation of Paradise. They do not for a moment advert to the grave contradiction this involves. Of the three attitudes it is the least excusable and perhaps the most frequent. It is one of the signs that faith has little or no influence where daily life is concerned, and that it will not be permitted to have such an influence. It is a symptom of unconscious flight in one who does not wish to face the problem. But it is no solution. Sooner or later the suppressed conflict will explode and then the remedy will probably arrive too late.

The Cause of the Difficulties

These attitudes in face of the problem do not seem very objective. An apparently insoluble dilemma appears between science and faith, common sense and traditional catechism. Some solve the problem by closing their eyes. Life already is full of so many

problems . . . ! There are two other approaches, but they both
suffer from the same defect: The Bible is wrong or science is
wrong—it is never considered that those who make such a judgment could be wrong. In fact the fundamental difficulty lies not in
the impossibility of reconciling faith and science on this or that
point, but rather in the way we see the text, in the preconceived
ideas we have before we even begin to read or interpret it.

So most of our problems with faith and science arise not from
faith or science but from the light in which we read the text. This
light has little to do with the Bible itself, but relates rather with the
way in which we today read and interpret the Bible. This depends
directly on our formation, which is the traditional, stereotyped
approach we described above, even if we do not realize it.

What is this light by which we read the Bible? What is this
traditional approach which predetermines our interpretation? It is
our habit of thinking of the Paradise narrative as an historico-
informative description. We read the text to get divinely guaranteed information about what happened at the beginning of the
history of the human race. We imagine that the text was written by
the author to give us this information.

This approach is the cause of our problems. It is, in fact, on this
historico-informative level that science is coming forward with
solidly based arguments contradicting the information given by the
Bible. This conflict goes back a long time. It began with Galileo.
But the Bible, as we shall see later in greater detail, approaches and
presents the story of Adam and Eve from a completely different
outlook. It has a different mind-set. It does not work on the
historico-informative level. If we do not recognize this we run the
risk of getting involved in all these contradictions. We make use of
the message in a way never intended by the author. The only way
we can avoid doing this is to change our "spectacles"—our way of
looking at the earthly Paradise. We are like a person of A.D. 3000
trying to read a twentieith-century novel as if it were an historico-
informative book. The reader could not help getting an erroneous
idea of the history of the twentieth century. He will keep on having
insurmountable difficulties until he finally decides to change his
approach.

CHAPTER TWO

Discovering the Biblical Point of View

When it speaks of Paradise, the primary concern of the Bible is not the past as past. It has no wish to give a detailed account of what happened back in the beginning of history. Rather its interest is in its readers, the writer's contemporaries. The text, with its description of Paradise and account of the sin of Adam and Eve, was elaborated with their concrete situation in mind. With a courage and a realism that provokes both admiration and imitation even today, the Bible here places itself in front of the actual situation of the people.

In the life of the people, something was out of joint. The future was endangered. If something were not done, utter chaos would be the inevitable result. The Paradise narrative is the confrontation with this drastic situation of the people. Even today, in the text itself, we can clearly see this confrontation as the motive. The aim of the Bible is not particularly nor primarily to give its readers information about what had happened in the past but rather about what was happening in their very lives. In this text its wish is to lead them towards taking a more critical stance in face of their reality—because of and by way of their faith in God.

The following six points summarize the point of view and purpose of the biblical narrative. Each will be treated at greater length later in our study.

1. In the light of his faith in God, the writer perceives a terrible situation which he wishes to *denounce* in unequivocal terms.

2. He is not satisfied with a generic denunciation but goes into precise responsibilities; he wants the reader to discover the *root cause* of the general malaise and to become aware of the *origin* of

this widespread and insidious evil; in other words he directs the reader's attention to the *original* sin. 3. He wants his brothers to *become aware* of the possibility that they might share the blame for this evil, especially since this sense of responsibility is as it were diluted or almost absent. 4. He wishes to awaken them to concrete and effective action, taking the evil at its root and so *transforming* the situation. 5. Finally, he *guarantees* that this transforming action is feasible since God's power, on which the change depends, is greater than the power that maintains the evil. 6. Thus the text reawakens hope, courage, and the ability to resist.

How can we be sure that the above is the point of view and purpose of the Paradise narrative? To really understand any book, it should be read in accordance with the intention of the author. A Dickens novel, for example, is automatically read as a novel. There is no need for an interview with the author nor need he put on the cover, "Take note! This is a novel!" The structure and literary form of the book itself reveals its genre just as it would if it were history or poetry. If some reader is deceived, the mistake is not to be attributed to the writer. It comes from ignorance on the part of the reader who cannot distinguish between one literary form and another, between novel and history; or it can come from the changes that occur from time to time in the way books are written.

So too the biblical text we are dealing with has a distinct literary form which leaves no doubt as to its purpose and genre; at least it left no doubt in the readers for whom it was intended. Since then, however, there have been many great changes in the way in which writers express their thoughts. We are no longer familiar with the ancient types of literary composition. So we run the risk of deceiving ourselves in their regard. And in fact we have deceived ourselves by reading the text as if it were a familiar literary form, when in reality the writer intended something entirely different. Thus the Paradise narrative became for us a kind of reporting which gave its readers an account of past events, for this is the literary form with which we are most familiar. In fact the text has a very different intent.

For this reason, our interpretation will be based on a detailed analysis of the biblical text. We have no wish to depart from the perspective and purpose proper to the narrative, thus running the risk of introducing lights and shades of meaning foreign to it. We will see how rich the text is in meaning and message, even for us of the twentieth century, and we will see how much we have impoverished it with our traditional viewpoint, characterized as it is by so much polemic.

The Central Idea

The Genesis (2:4–3:25) narrative has three distinct parts. They resemble the great architectonic lines of an art work which connect the different parts and give unity to the work as a whole. Through them the central idea diffuses itself into every detail of the finished product.

1. *Genesis* 2:4–25
The creation of Paradise and of man; man is placed in Paradise. Brought out here is the Creator's intention for the world and for man.

2. *Genesis* 3:1–7
Sin of the man and the woman. This passage describes how the transition is made from the ideal situation of Paradise to the real situation of everyday experience.

3. *Genesis* 3:8–24
Divine chastisement, brought on by the sin. In the description of this chastisement, the reader recognizes the common, daily situation of his own human existence.

This division reveals a very precise objective: to clarify for the reader his concrete life situation, dominated by sufferings, pains, doubts, and death, so well described in the *third* part. Where are we to look for the cause of this general malaise? Other peoples were of the opinion that all this was due to the influence of the gods. For this reason they fell into a fatalistic passivity when confronted with the evils of life. What use would it be to react, when the origin of the evils was beyond the control of man? The

Bible, however, does not subscribe to this way of thinking. It knows that the good and just God would never make so wretched a world. Its God would want the exact opposite. The ideal that God would want for man is described in the *first* part. It is Paradise. Within the narrative, the Paradise ideal acts as a counter-reflection that sets itself in contrast, point by point, with the ambiguous reality of the present world, as described in the *third* part. But if God is not responsible for this widespread evil of the world and of life, who *is* responsible?

The answer is given in the *second* part. The one responsible is the ADAM, man himself, and no other. The root of the evils is in him. So it is not permissable to have an attitude of passivity or of fatalism in the face of the evils of life. If man, by *his own* fault, provoked these evils, then—and here is yet another objective of the narrative—the same man, by *his* conversion and initiative, can bring about the elimination of the evil and reach the ideal of Paradise. Every effort in this direction will be successful, since the will of God has not changed. It has always remained unaltered, desiring Paradise and planning that man should be there. And so, upheld by the power and the faithfulness of God, man is reborn to hope.

This is the central idea of the narrative and it dictated the formulation of the various parts. In the literary exposition of his ideas, the author inverted the way by which he himself arrived, with the help of God, at the faith intuition he describes. In his personal reflections, he set out from the ambiguous and painful life of the people, to arrive at a discovery of what really was the will of God about human life. He formulated his discovery by using the image of the ideal of Paradise. In his literary exposition, he starts with the ideal of Paradise, hoping to bring the reader to the ambiguous reality of his daily life, with which he terminates the narrative in the third part. And so he brings his contemporaries to a rejection of this reality as something normal and natural, seeing it rather as a situation contrary to the will of God, so clearly expressed in the description of Paradise. They should stop, look, judge, and start to react.

The starting point of the author of the narrative was the reflec-

tion on the evils of life. What were those evils that the Bible wishes
to denounce?

Awareness of Evil

The perception of evil depends, to a large degree, on the level
of culture. Everybody does not have the same critical awareness
with regard to the evils he suffers. Lack of water is an evil for us,
but not to the same extent as for the Bedouin who lives in the
desert. A stone in one's shoe is an inconvenience only for one who
wears shoes. To be without glass in the window is an affliction for
one who lives in a civilized environment, but not for the Indian in
his wigwam. Wild animals are a real danger for the one who lives in
the wilds, but not for those who live in civilized regions. And so we
could go on multiplying examples.

Evil becomes a problem the moment it passes the limit of being
bearable. At that moment, man begins to ask himself: "Why must
I put up with this?" But there are many evils that have not yet
reached that limit. We tolerate them in the most natural way
imaginable, since we think of them as an integral part of life. Thus
we bear with the heat of summer and the cold of winter. Nobody
revolts against this, saying, "Why must man suffer cold and
heat?" Today, nobody is satisfied with an insufficient salary, but
salary itself is tolerated and accepted as a natural and integral part
of life. It is quite possible that in the future, as man's awareness
grows, we may reach the point of no longer tolerating that kind of
mutual dependence implied in a salary. So there are many things in
life which we consider natural and normal today but which will one
day be declared incompatible with human living, for example, the
school institution as a normal system of formation, urban centers
with their huge agglomeration of human beings, high-rise apart-
ments, large churches that are empty six days a week, and so forth.

The greater the degree of sensitivity, education, culture, and
progress, the quicker one reaches one's limit of tolerance, and the
more likely are the evils of life to pass from being simply an integral
part of life to being a problem demanding a solution. This is what is
called critical awareness in the face of reality.

Thus, the perception of evils as *evils* is very relative. Critical awareness depends on the culture, progress, way of life, sensitivity of the person or group. It can come to life and grow in a right or wrong direction. It depends on the vision that one has of man. For this reason, the faith that animates greatly influences the formation of critical awareness.

The above should help give a better understanding of the biblical narrative we are about to explain. The evil denounced by the biblical author was seen by him within the cultural limits of that time, in keeping with the degree of awareness and the way of life of the people, in the light of their faith in God.

EVILS IN FAMILY LIFE

The author discerns a widespread ambiguity and contradiction in human life. What ought to be a good for man was really a cause and an instrument of suffering and oppression. Perhaps many do not perceive this, or may even regard it as something natural and inevitable. The author, however, no longer accepts it; he opposes it. In some ways, his critical awareness is much more evolved than ours today, since he was already refusing to accept certain things that have not even reached problem proportions for us. All of this he describes in the third part of his narrative.

Ambiguity of human love. Human love between husband and wife, a thing so good and beautiful, has in reality become an instrument of domination. The woman feels herself drawn to the man and at the same time dominated by him. "You will be drawn to your husband and he will dominate you" (Gen. 3:16). Love is ambiguous. Why?

Ambiguity of life itself. Life itself is ambiguous. Everything in Man cries out, "I want to live!" But in spite of this, death inevitably awaits him. Nobody escapes: "You will return to the earth, for from it you were drawn. Dust you are! Dust you are going to remain!" (Gen. 3:19). Why this germ of death within life itself, casting a veil of sadness over all our joys?

Ambiguity of maternity. Each new generation of children, perpetuating life, increasing joy among men, arrives inexplicably amid the pains of childbirth. Why? Should it not be the opposite? Maternity makes a slave out of woman, multiplying her sufferings: "I must indeed multiply your sufferings; you will have to become pregnant often and it is with pains that you will bring forth your children" (Gen. 3:16). For the woman who becomes a mother, death draws near each time life begins for the other. Why?

Ambiguity of the earth. The earth, destined to produce fruits and food for man, produces only "briars and thorns" (Gen. 3:18). Its soil seems to be accursed (*cf.* Gen. 3:17). It resists the work of man. It is only as a result of much suffering that he can draw from it a little food for sustenance: "Only with great difficulty will you succeed in drawing from it your sustenance, all of your life long . . . You will have to sweat to be able to eat your bread" (Gen. 3:17,19). Why all this? Why is the earth not as it ought to be?

Ambiguity of work. Work, a necessary part of human life and a way of providing sustenance, is, in reality, a cause of much suffering and weariness, since it demands much effort for little return. Difficulties, sweat, fatigue, and in the end, death. (Gen. 3:17,19). Why?

Ambiguity of the animals. The animals, creatures inferior to man, should live in peace with him and should serve him. Instead, he cannot trust them. They are a threat to human life and there is a deadly enmity between men and animals (Gen. 3:15). This is a real problem for those who live far from civilization, isolated, where treacherous serpents lie in wait for man at every step. Why does life combat life?

Ambiguity of religion. God, as Creator and friend of man, should be a reason for joy and hope. To be able to live with God ought to be the supreme good. In reality, however, his presence causes fear. Man runs away and hides: "I heard your footsteps in the garden, but I was afraid, because I am naked. And I went to hide" (Gen. 3:10). Why?

Why all this? The biblical author has reached a degree of awareness at which all these things have ceased to be a simple, natural, integral part of human life. The realism of his faith in God has called into question the reality of existence, has recognized these contradictions and ambiguities and cannot bear them any longer. Life would be more life were it not for the terrible ambiguity that pervades everything. The author begins to react, seeking the why of all this.

The author's range of observation, at least in this narrative, is very restricted. It is the environment of family and farm; love and marriage; pains of childbirth and work in the house with the children; living and dying; the dry earth and the field to be planted with hard work, at the price of the sweat of one's brow; the threat of wild animals in the hinterland; the religiosity of fear. In all probability the author is a peasant, one of those wise realists who began the proverbs, later to be compiled into the books of wisdom. So it was while he lived in this rural atmosphere that he progressed in his experience of life, and began to evolve a critical awareness of his reality.

EVILS IN SOCIAL LIFE

The author did not keep to the limits of his own backyard, as if he were the only person in the world. His family life does not exist as something distinct from the wider social life. The two interpenetrate; one has an influence on the other and together they produce a unity. So, in chapters four to eleven the author casts a critical look at the world around him. In this wider circle, he discerns other evils and ambiguities and goes on to describe them.

The Paradise narrative cannot be separated from the chapters that follow it. The literary unity that links the first eleven chapters of Genesis reflects the real unity of individual, family, and social life.

Domination of violence and vengeance. There exists an extremity of violence in human living, where Cain kills Abel (Gen. 4:8). Violence is so great as to become a social plague. The only way to protect oneself against it is redoubled violence and repression. But vengeance and repression all too frequently go beyond just limits. Any little row leads to a vengeance that repays seven times seventy: ''I killed a man for wounding me, a boy for striking me. Sevenfold vengeance is taken for Cain, but seventy-sevenfold for Lamech." (Gen. 4:24). Violence continues to spread among men, while men, being all of the same human race, could be friends. Why?

Domination of magic.   Living in a situation in which he is always on the defensive and threatened, man looks for support from superior and divine forces. He enters the world of superstition and magic, seeking by means of magic rites and actions to guarantee his life and to gain the protection of the gods. Divine and human are so confused that the end is sacred prostitution, and the pretended alliance of the sons of God with the daughters of men (Gen. 6:1–2,4). Men lose their sense of proportion and everything falls into a state of widespread corruption (Gen. 6:5). Why all this? Why not live in faith and trust, the qualities by which man places himself in his correct place before the divinity, which allows him to grow and realize himself.

Universal domination of division.   Finally, the author perceives that in this world nobody agrees. All live in mutual combat, each in his own corner, without a chance of unity, even if they desire it, because of distance and language differences (Gen. 11:9). The world offers a picture of inexplicable confusion and division, when humanity could offer a display of unity. It is the will to dominate, one over the other, that causes this division. Men arrive at the conclusion that they need not render an account to anything or anybody. They are the sole lords of all. The result is general confusion. Why?

The above is the critical analysis of social reality made by the biblical author. He uses the ordinary, everyday language and categories of the time. He speaks of these problems just as they appeared at that time. Violence, vengeance, magic, corruption, universal division, and domination—all appeared in much more primitive guise than they do today. Besides, the rural author seems to have a certain misgiving about technical progress and posits these vices—vengeance, violence, divisive domination—as vices of those who live in cities (Gen. 11:4); those who work with iron and copper (Gen. 4:22); those who live as nomads in the desert

(Gen. 4:20), among whom we find strange groups of musical artists (Gen. 4:21). Already, rural dwellers were showing signs of being conservatives, wrapped up in their own class. But this did not keep them from having a critical awareness of reality. Technical progress on the one hand and critical awareness on the other do not always go together.

CHAPTER THREE

The Pedagogy of the Bible
in Denouncing Evils

The way of presenting the reality of individual, family, and social life as described in the foregoing chapter is an attempt to communicate to others the critical awareness which the author already has. He wishes to open their eyes, drawing them from apathy and awakening them to the problem which that reality involves: the problem of finding the cause of all these ills, in order to combat them efficiently.

There is a certain pedagogy in this effort at conscientization. All the problems are not thrown at the reader at once. The critical awareness begins with a minute observation of what is individual and personal, within the proximate environment of the intimacy of family life. Only afterwards, moving on from this, does it begin to widen its horizons until it reaches the universal and collective problems of humanity.

The Bible thus makes it clear that personal life and world problems are inseparably linked. It thus avoids the pretension of those who seek to mend the world without first submitting their own personal and family life to a serious overhaul.

It should be noted, too, that the first eleven chapters of Genesis, including the Paradise narrative, are in no way statistical. By this we mean that they are not and do not pretend to be an objective account of a critical investigation of reality. They already represent a later phase, in which the results of a critical observation of reality are used with a view to provoking a change. The end that the Bible envisages is not simply to give information about the situation in which the readers live, but to bring the readers to an awareness of the real situation in which they find

themselves, with a view to its transformation. Many not only do
not know this real situation but even contribute to an increase in
the reigning confusion. The narrative awakens them to the risk
they are running if they continue along present lines. It is essen-
tially a nonconformist narrative of one who has already made his
choice in face of reality. He has made this option based on his faith
in God.

Forming a Critical Awareness

Why doesn't the author conform to the evils and ambiguities
that he noted in his family life and in the life of society? How did he
come to have this peculiar vision which he expressed in his narrative?

It is because of the realism of his faith. It is because of the
conviction of the author and of the whole Bible that God is good
and just. God wills the good of men and not their condemnation.
We cannot attribute to God the blame for the evils we suffer.
Neither can we say, "Patience, let's just bear it. That's life! That's
the way God wills it!" The author would be the last to seek in God
or in religion an excuse for a false patience that would compromise
with the situation. His faith tells him: "God does not want this
reality!" On this point he disagrees radically with the other peoples, who attribute all evils to the direct action of the gods. Not he.
What is around us could not have the blessing of God nor his
approval. Neither can it be maintained under the pretext that God
wishes it so.

He communicates this critical vision of reality by saying that
the situation in which the people and humanity find themselves is a
situation of *punishment* (*cf.* Gen. 3:14–19). Since it is a situation of
punishment, the person punished is the one responsible for it. He
cannot withdraw into himself, ignoring his share of responsibility
for the evils we suffer. Besides, a situation of punishment is never a
normal and definitive situation. It is merely provisory and transi-
tory. Its abnormality will last as long as the punishment is not
fulfilled and the fault expiated. One cannot say: "It is God's
punishment; so God wills this situation! All we can do is be
patient!" The judge who judges and sentences the accused to a

punishment does not want the punishment to become a permanent situation. On the contrary, he seeks the good of the accused. This good is beyond the punishment. Indeed, it can only be achieved through the active and responsible acceptance of the punishment. At the root of the punishment lies the fault of the person being punished, from which there resulted a breakdown in relationship between persons which demands to be reestablished. Only by a positive acceptance of the punishment can the condemned man redeem himself, rehabilitate himself, and restore the interrupted relationship.

Since the human situation is one of punishment, two attitudes in the face of life's evils are definitely excluded: passivity and revolt. To be in prison is a punishment which envisages rehabilitation. The prisoner will not be rehabilitated if he revolts against his imprisonment; nor will he if he merely accepts it passively. The punishment should lead him to a deepening of his life and a consideration of his fault and his responsibility.

Where there exists a fatalistic view of life, there is no place for punishment, nor for regeneration or redemption. In saying that the unfortunate situation of man is a situation of punishment inflicted by God, the Bible simply appeals to responsibility and encourages each person to ask, "What is my share of blame in all this? How am I to face up to this punishment in a way that will redeem and rehabilitate me, making me become once more what God wants me to be?" Excluded is the passive acceptance of reality and the blind revolt against it, since by both of these attitudes, man denies his responsibility for the evils of life. Both are attitudes of alienation.

Finally, by saying that the evils we suffer are a punishment from God, the Bible makes the relationship of man with God the fundamental basis for the harmony of everything else. The disrupted order of life cannot be restored without considering the place God ought to occupy in the life of men.

In this approach to reality, two fundamental questions arise: 1. It is easy to say that God does not want the world to be as it is. But how then *does* he want it to be? 2. The judge who pronounces the sentence is not the cause of the evil. He merely pronounces over the guilty one that which he has called down on himself by his bad conduct. But what then *is* this crime which we committed and for which we are suffering all these evils?

The reply to these two questions will bring us to an understanding of the meaning of Paradise and the sin of Adam.

The Launching Pad of the Idea of Paradise

His faith in God turns the author into an aware person who does not merely conform to the situation. Instead of leading him to a conformist fatalism, it leads him to resist, to react, to seek a solution. It leads him to stimulate and help others to have the same degree of awareness as himself. His faith is neither that of the fatalist, nor the providentialist faith of one who hopes for everything from God, without any participation on the part of man. His reasoning runs thus: If the world as it is, is not as God wishes it to be, then I, in all good conscience, cannot contribute to its continuing as it is. That would be for me to act against the will of God.

But what is this will of God? If the world is wrong, if it should be transformed to be in keeping with the will of God, then I should know quite concretely what it is that God wants with regard to the world and life. If not, then I can do nothing, since I do not know how to direct my activity.

The author, obviously, does not know how the world ought to be to conform to the will of God. There is no evidence that he had an interview with God on this subject. He knows only this erring world and no other. But he does know that God is good, just, and true. This faith conviction of his about God is the launching pad of his message. It is precisely because of it that he is convinced that the actual situation is not as it ought to be. A good, just, and true God would never make such a world, nor could he ask for the passive acceptance of such a world. But how then should it be?

To answer this question and to bring about a clearer appreciation of what man is losing by his wrong conduct, the author simply imagines a situation of well-being from which he eliminates all the evil he sees and opposes in the world in which he lives. The result of this intellectual exercise is *Paradise*. Paradise describes a life situation exactly the opposite of that which the author knows and experiences in the reality of everyday life. It suffices to analyze his description of Paradise, comparing it with what we saw above about the real life situation, to be convinced that this is the intention of the narrative. One situation is the negative, the other the positive; but both refer to the same photograph, to the same human life.

Paradise: The Reverse Image of Reality

Analyzing, part by part, the description of Paradise in Gen. 2:4–25, we note the clear intention of establishing an opposition-parallel with the real life situation described in the third part (Gen. 3:8–24).

Husband-Wife relationship.   The wife is not dominated by the husband but is his equal companion. God wants her to be "one who helps the man and can converse with him" (Gen. 2:18). And the man recognizes this dignity and equality, for he exclaims, "This is bone of my bones and flesh of my flesh" (Gen. 2:23). The man is attracted to the woman and unites himself with her, "the two becoming one thing" (Gen. 2:24), without one dominating the other.

Life and death.   Life does not end in death, since it can last forever. But it lasts forever, not by a dynamism proper to and inherent in life itself, but by a free gift of God. Immortality is not within the natural scope of man, no matter how much he might desire it. But God responded to the deep desire of man and "caused the tree of life to grow in the middle of the orchard" (Gen. 2:9). The man need only eat to be able to live forever (*cf.* Gen. 3:22). Death has been eliminated and no longer saddens life.

Maternity and pains of childbirth.   Here there are no pains of childbirth, since there is no childbirth. Since man does not die, there is no need to procreate to prolong life beyond death. The situation has arrived of which Jesus will later speak: "At the resurrection men and women do not marry" (Matt. 22:30). He announces the end of procreation since a situation has developed in which men "can no longer die" (Luke 20:36). What continues to exist is perfect love. The author, by all appearances, is not thinking of one historical couple at the beginning of the whole human race. He is thinking, as we shall see, of the men and women of his time whom he knows, all symbolized and represented by Adam and Eve.

Fertility of the earth.   The earth is no longer accursed. It is fertile and produces leafy trees with an abundance of fruits of every kind: "beautiful and tasty fruits" (Gen. 2:9), which guarantee man's sustenance. There is no drought, since irrigation is naturally assured by a river which "waters the orchard and then divides into four" (Gen. 2:10). They are the four greatest rivers of the world of that time. Such a great abundance of water could not exist in any part of the world. And here too the Bible stresses that man was not born into this situation but is placed in it by God (Gen. 2:8, 15). All this man will possess through a gift of God, who places it freely within man's capacity.

Work and sustenance.   Work is no longer a reason for oppression. It is part of the life of man, but it is light work: to cultivate an orchard and take care of it (Gen. 2:15). This does not require much effort, especially since the orchard has plenty of water and only trees grow in it. It is work anybody would be delighted to do.

Relationship with the animals.   There is no longer any enmity between men and animals. Quite the contrary. The animals exist for man and are what the man wishes them to be: "The man gave purpose and name to all the animals and birds and to all the creatures that live in the undergrowth" (Gen. 2:20).

The Man before God.   God is a friend to men and lives with them in the greatest intimacy, without his presence being a reason for fear or disquiet. He strolls in the orchard where they live (Gen. 3:8–10). He is surprised by the behavior of the man who flees in fear (Gen. 3:9–11). He had never done that before.

This is what the author imagines and thus he makes concrete God's intention for the world and for men. In words that are simple and popular but of great depth and seriousness, he was able to present the ideal that God wishes to realize. It is the ideal of total harmony: harmony of man with God; harmony of man with his fellow-men; harmony with the animal kingdom; harmony of man with the nature around him. It is a radical and total order. Everything is perfectly integrated around the central axis: man's friendship with God. There is no dissonant voice.

The picture presented here by the author in his description of Paradise is the exact opposite of the chaos and disorder he is familiar with, which he experiences and suffers in daily life. All that he denounces in his description of family life has no place here. It has been eliminated. In paradise there is no ambiguity, no oppression or domination. There is total peace. Thus the author concretizes his faith in the goodness, the power, the faithfulness of God.

CHAPTER FOUR

Paradise as Prophecy

As the author pictures it, the world is not as God would like it to be. God does not want the husband to dominate, the wife to suffer the pains of childbirth; he does not want drought or death; he does not want the slavery or oppression of work nor the threat of animals; he does not want a religion of fear. And God does not and will not change his mind. Once he has willed Paradise, i.e., once he has willed perfect harmony and total peace, he keeps on pursuing this objective until in fact it is realized. "He spoke, and it was created, he commanded, and there it stood. Yahweh thwarts the plans of nations, frustrates the intentions of peoples; but Yahweh's plans hold good forever, the intentions of his heart from age to age" (Ps. 33:9–11).

This will of God who desires good and peace is, for the biblical author, the guarantee that Paradise continues to be a real possibility. Trusting in this sovereign will of God, man can go to work, can begin to resist the evils of life and work to build a world of peace. His efforts will bear fruit. He will be able to say, "Happy the nation whose God is Yahweh, the people he has chosen for his heritage" (Ps. 33:12). For the author, Paradise is not something that belongs to the past but rather something of the future. It is not a nostalgia that had left its mark on man, stirring up in him the desire to return to the hiding place of his mother's womb. Quite the opposite. Paradise is, as it were, the mock-up of the world. It is the construction plan to be realized by the contractor who is man. It is a project that is a constant challenge to the faith and courage of man. It is put at the beginning of the Bible, because before anybody makes anything, he should know what he wants; he should elaborate a project capable of being executed. The full realization is expressed in anticipation in the description of Paradise, with images and symbols drawn from the reality of the people of that time, to serve as an orientation and stimulus for on-going human action.

Because of this, it may be said that Paradise is a prophecy, projected into the past. In fact, parts of this description may be found also in the books of the prophets. The author did not speak a language foreign to the people, but used images and symbols that everybody knew. Thus, for example, the prophet Ezekiel speaks of "the Garden of God" and of "Eden, the Garden of God" (Ezek. 31:7–9,16,18; 36:35). For Isaiah, Eden, the Garden of Yahweh, serves as an image of the future of the city of Zion (Isa. 51:3). In the same book of the prophet Isaiah, the messianic future is described as a situation of total peace between men and animals (Isa. 11:6–9). The description of the future as a condition of perfect friendship between God and men is frequent in the books of the prophets (cf. Jer. 24:7; 32:39; 31:34). Because of this friendship with God, sins will all be pardoned (Jer. 31:34). Everything will be renewed (Isa. 66:22; 65:17). All the evils of life will disappear (Isa. 11:9).

Other elements of this narrative of Paradise are to be found in the same prophetic books and in other parts of the Bible. Jeremiah uses the image of God the Potter: "As clay is in the hands of the potter, so you are in mine, House of Israel" (Jer. 18:6). The image of the tree of life occurs in the Book of Proverbs. (Prov. 11:30; 13:12; 15:4). Isaiah speaks of the desire to be equal to God (cf. Gen. 3:5), which brought death as a punishment (Isa. 14:14–15). Ezekiel recounts a similar story about someone who was put in the Garden of God and was expelled because of his sin (Ezek. 28:17–19).

The author did just as the prophets did. With well-known literary elements he forged an image of the future which he projected onto the past. God did as the architect does. Before building a house, an architect elaborates the ideal project. The ideal is always first in intention and last in execution. It *exists* before any concrete action and serves to orient action during the execution phase until the end is reached.

Man's Hope: Supernatural
and Preternatural Gifts

The Paradise narrative suggests the enormous possibilities placed in human life by God, possibilities that remain open today. For man there exists the real possibility of being able to really live with God, without any sin, in perfect justice. Man, as God wishes him to be, has besides this the real possibility of living forever—of being immortal. Finally, there is open to him a way of being happy one day, without suffering, living completely integrated with himself, with others, and with nature. This is the hope which man can nourish within his heart and which ought to be the spur to his activity.

These possiblities, however, are not within man as a natural part of his life. They are a free gift of God, traditionally called "supernatural and preternatural gifts." By means of them, God has enlarged the horizon of human existence. Through this narrative, the Bible puts man in a somewhat higher place, allowing him to rise above the narrow horizons of his own capacity. It allows man to look a little farther into the future God has in store for him and thus orient himself better in the present. In a word, the author lets it be known that the destiny of man lies in total harmony, and that man, helped by the power and faithfulness of God, can *realize* future peace. God has put everything into man's hands. The world will be what he makes of it.

Thus any action for the building of peace, for the preservation of life, or for harmony among men, has the blessing of God and will be vindicated in the future, even though man does not see clearly how this will come about. He is asked to make an act of faith and place his trust in God. Paradise is a way of helping man to reach such an attitude of faith; it opens up his life to a new hope and can awaken in him a total commitment to the cause of peace.

Reality Contradicts God's Ideal:
Who Is Responsible?

With his description of Paradise, the author denounces, root and branch, the world he knows. The reader recognizes in it without any difficulty the opposite of what he lives and experiences in everyday life. Reading this description produces an impact and provokes the big question: "But if this is the world God wants, why then is our world the exact opposite of what it ought to be? Who is responsible for this?

With this question, the problem is brought to the surface and will never return to the subconscious, since it will stimulate man to keep on trying until he gets a satisfactory answer. This question is the first step towards creating in man a critical awareness. It is the first step towards *conversion* or the transformation the Bible wants to bring about.

The answer will be given in the pages which follow concerning the serpent who tempts the woman and leads the Man and Woman to transgress God's command. In this description, the author tries to pinpoint the *origin of evil* and to enlighten the reader with regard to his responsibilities for the evils of life. He tries to show where sin lies. He speaks what may be for us a strange language but one perfectly understandable for his readers, since he uses the common elements and symbols of the culture of his day.

Two elements play a key role in the solution of the problem which is upsetting him: the first is the two trees, one of life and the other of knowledge of good and evil; the second is the serpent.

THE TREE OF KNOWLEDGE OF GOOD AND EVIL

The only prohibition affecting man in Paradise is that he may not eat of the tree of knowledge of good and evil: "On the day that you eat from it, it is certain that you will die" (Gen. 2:17). This may seem to resemble a prohibition arbitrarily saying, "On the day that you fail to heed a red traffic signal, you will be condemned to death, you and all your descendants!" In reality however, it is not like that.

The order of God is not just a prohibition but rather has two facets: It permits eating from all the trees, including the tree of life, and it forbids eating from the tree of knowledge of good and evil (Gen. 2:16–17). These two divine orientations cannot be separated, since one is the alternative of the other. This is the option between life and death, left to the free choice of man. On the one side is the tree of life, and on the other the tree of knowledge of good and evil which brings death.

For a good understanding of the thought of the author, one must consider the close link and quasi-identification between the Wisdom and the Law of God, both symbolized by a tree. The tree was a familiar image of the wisdom communicated by God to man. The one who has met Wisdom has met life (Prov. 8:35). So it used to be said of Wisdom that it was a "tree of life" (Prov. 3:18). It taught the way to be followed in life. It indicated the turns and intersections at which man should be careful in order to avoid evil and to do good. The most perfect expression of this Wisdom is to be met with in the Law of God (*cf*. Ps. 119:98,104,130). By following the wise prescriptions of the law, man would find life: "By these you have kept me alive" (Ps. 119:93). The man who observed the Law became like a luxuriant tree, planted at the edge of a stream (Ps. 1:3; Jer. 17:8).

Thus, true knowledge of good and evil could only be obtained by the conquest of Wisdom, that is, by observance of the Law of God. On this depended the free choice between life and death. At the moment that he handed over the *Law* to the people, Moses said, "See, today I set . . . before you life and prosperity, death and disaster. I set before you life or death, blessing or curse. Choose life, then, so that you and your descendants may live, in the love of Yahweh your God, obeying his voice, clinging to him" (Deut. 30:15, 19–20). Thus the one who observes the Law of God eats of the tree of life and gains life. He obtains "a heart to understand how to discern between good and evil" (1 Kings 3:9).

But man is free to reject the Law of God with his Wisdom. He can try to get life and the knowledge of good and evil on his own, without bothering about any higher norm. This would be like somebody lost in an unknown region who concocted a map of the region out of his own mind and then took his bearings from it to find his way. The map would be no more than a projection of his own ideas and desires. It would not offer any guarantee. To trust in it would be sheer illusion. Thus is the man who follows his own criterion and makes for himself his own law without bothering with the Law of God, seeking to be his own unique, exclusive, and

absolute criterion for his behavior. Such a man could find everything, except God and life. He would continue lost in the unknown
regions of life. This would be the most complete illusion. He would
find no exit. Inevitably, he would meet death. The one who acts in
this way falls into the category of those of whom Isaiah speaks:
"Woe to those who call evil good, and good evil, who substitute
darkness for light and light for darkness. . . . Woe to those who
think themselves *wise* and believe themselves cunning" (Isa.
5:20–21). This is the condition of the man who has become closed
up into himself and has ceased to think of his life as a gift received.
He thinks of his life as his own exclusive property, without any
relationship to a higher value outside of himself. This would be to
kill man, to cut him off at the root. We do not need even to appeal to
the Bible to realize that man does not find the meaning of his life
only within himself, but rather outside of himself, in the other. The
problem is to know: which other? The Bible tells us that the Other,
the one who can really be the definitive end of all man's anxiety,
without danger of frustration, is God.

Thus man is faced with two alternatives, made explicit in the
order of God: either attain wisdom by observing the Law of God
and so find life in him; or, ignoring all this, try to be a god for
himself (*cf.* Gen. 3:5), by deciding for himself and by means of his
own research what is good and evil and so find death by cutting
himself off from God.

This is the meaning of God's order to eat of all the trees,
including the tree of life, and not to eat of the tree of knowledge of
good and evil. These are the two options with which man is faced.
It has nothing to do with a period of trial during which man's
obedience would be tested. It is the very condition of human life:
to be able to dispose of everything, but to dispose according to the
wisdom and the design of the Creator. This divine order is a
symbol that summarizes the norm which ought to regulate all
behavior: "Be wise and follow the Law of God, i.e., eat of the tree
of life. Do not try to build a law for yourself from your own head,
i.e., do not eat of the forbidden fruit of the tree of knowledge of
good and evil." This is not an arbitrary order. It is an expression of
the fundamental law inscribed in the very existence of man.[3]

Intermezzo on creative action.   Our notion of creation is defined as *creation from nothing.* In the Bible it is not so. The ancients looked at creation from a different point of view. Looking at life, they perceived a constant rhythm that guaranteed their sustenance: rain in the spring, regular flooding of the rivers, the inalterable round of the seasons of the year, succession of day and night, and annual renewal of the flock. A force greater than man seemed to maintain this harmonious order and to keep away at every moment the threat of disorder and chaos which would place life in danger. Human life remained in total dependence on this order-maintaining force.

Inquiry at that time into the origin of the universe did not go beyond the recognition of this order. It was with the creation of harmony, they thought, that all things began to be. Without this, nothing could exist. Thus they identified the creative order with the order-maintaining force. So for them the situation anterior to creation was not our *nothingness*, but was chaos or universal disorder, in which human life was not possible (*cf.* Gen. 2:4–6).

This disorder, however, does not seem to have been definitively overcome by the creative action. Life was constantly endangered by the unforeseen threats of nature, upsetting the rhythm of the universe: violent storms, disastrous floods, earthquakes, prolonged droughts, sickness among the flocks. The supreme ideal would be to arrive at such a condition of harmony and peace that there would no longer be any threat of disorder and chaos.

For the other peoples, this constant threat was attributed to the action of evil gods. Because of this, they tried to pacify these gods by means of magic and superstitious cult. For them, the way to reach the ideal of harmony lay in magic cult and superstitious practices. This way did not touch on man's life or ethical behavior.

But the Bible is not of this way of thinking. For it, the threat against order came from man himself, when he refused to follow the way indicated by the Law of God. The way to reach the ideal of harmony and peace did not lie in a magic cult, cut off from life, but was a way to be opened by man himself, by means of an ethical behavior motivated by his faith in God. Only by following that way would it be possible to reintegrate life from the roots and build the order of which Paradise was the symbol.

The norm of this ethical behavior would be Law and Wisdom. What God wished was not an alienating cult but a taking on of life: to eat of the tree of life and to stop eating of the tree of knowledge of good and evil.

Thus we see that the narrative of Genesis 2:4—3:24 has little to do with the initial creation of the world and of man. It has to do with the re-creation of peace and harmony, to be brought about by the conscious collaboration of man.

The origin of life's evils lies in not wanting to take on life as we should. For the author, the Law of God, understood not as a fence placed around life to enclose liberty, but as a source of wisdom and as an orientation for the future, is the instrument of true *order* and true *progress*. Its observance leads to the conquest of peace and life. The future existence of Paradise will depend on this attitude of fidelity and obedience of man before God. There lies the central axis of things.

This law, formulated initially in the ten commandments, is, as it were, the first redaction of the "Declaration of the Rights of Man," and not only of his rights but also of his duties. The Hebrew people took this law as Constitution, constituting a People. They took it as the expression of the will and the wisdom of God.

To follow this Law implies that man recognizes his human condition as a man made from the clay of the earth (*cf.* Gen. 2:7). That is, he accepts and takes on his condition of total depedence on God. Man does not hold his life in his hands as his exclusive property. His life is a gift received, a job to be done. The life of man is, as it were, a vessel of clay, which breaks easily. This is the condition of man which he ought to accept if he wishes to be realistic.

Man's eternal temptation is that he does not want to recognize himself as a creature before God; it is to revolt against this condition of radical dependence and to seek to overcome his own limits by making himself a god (*cf.* Gen. 3:5), and by considering himself the unique, exclusive, and absolute norm of life and of good and evil. The root of sin is in the erroneous choice or option which man makes before God. He refuses to put himself in his rightful place before his Creator (*cf.* Ezek. 28:2–19).

By means of the Paradise narrative, the Bible wished to recall the attention of its readers to this aspect of human life. There was no order or peace because the people were abandoning the Law of God. Paradise had not been realized because they were eating of the forbidden fruit, abusing their liberty before God, thus prejudicing, perhaps without realizing it, their own well-being and happiness. For the author, the *original sin,* i.e., the origin of all the evils he noted and opposed, should be sought in disobedience to the Law of God. In other words, it should be sought in the refusal of men to take responsibility for their lives as they ought.

THE SERPENT, SYMBOL OF THE EVIL
THAT DRAWS MAN AWAY FROM GOD

But why were men abandoning the way of the Law of God and Wisdom, thus introducing chaos and disorder into every sector of human life? It was the *Serpent* who was attracting and tempting them. What exactly is this Serpent?

In the first place, for the Hebrew people, as for all of us, the serpent was a perverse and treacherous animal. One could not trust him. Everyone has an instinctive fear of this animal. He is loathsome and endangers life (*cf.* Gen. 49:17; Isa. 14:29; Job. 20:16; Prov. 23:32). Moreover, the serpent was a symbol of the Canaanite religion. The Canaanites were a people already living in Palestine before the arrival of the Hebrews. They had their own religion made up of rites centered on the fertility cult. The relationship with the divinity was exclusively in terms of ritual ceremonies and observances. It did not include any ethical demand. It did not influence life in any way as a transforming power. Such a religion was much more agreeable than the hard demands of the Law of God, since it even succeeded in making prostitution official and sacral, turning it into a rite and a sacred action. Prostitution was seen and practiced as a magic and superstitious attempt to conquer death and possess life. The Serpent was the symbol of all this conglomeration of magic, linked with the feritlity cult and prostitution. The identification was so great that the word *nagash* was used to signify both *serpent* and *to practice magic* (*cf.* Lev. 19:26; Deut. 18:10). For the Hebrew people, magic was forbidden as being the exact opposite of the attitude of faith and ethical commitment which God demanded from his people. Yet this type of religion never ceased to attract the people of God to an easier life. The great danger and the great temptation of the people was this very *Serpent*. He led the people to take refuge in rite and to abandon the hard demands of the Law of God. He led them to seek life, immortality, and the protection of God, not in a constant fidelity which would demand abandonment, trust, and courage, but in rites and promises which might appear to give greater security, since they gave man the impression that he was manipulating the power of God for his own benefit.

This Serpent was the great danger for the people. There were many who listened to his voice and let themselves be deceived by him, eating the forbidden fruit and abandoning the Law of God (*cf.* Gen. 3:1–5). There lay the *origin* of all evils, and a start must be made to attack evil at its root.

The symbol of the Serpent also appears in the pagan mythology of the time, as when he stole from Gilgamesh the plant or tree of life. Traces of this mythology are to be found in the Bible, where the Serpent is called Leviathan and is presented as the symbol of evil, the adversary of God who wishes good (*cf.* Ps. 74:14; 104:26; Isa. 27:1; Job 40:25–32; 41:1–26). But in the Bible the power of this adversary is neutralized. God is his superior and dominates him totally. Thus the image of the Serpent began in a general way to be the symbol of the forces of evil which took on different shapes in each epoch. In the time of the author the forces of evil were concretized in the magic religion of the Canaanites, a real temptation to divert the people from the true way of life.

This is the vision of reality offered by the Bible to its readers. Through this presentation it leads its readers and hearers to a serious revision of life. It is a call to reality. They should open their eyes. It makes them see how life, the actual condition of the people, the world, family and social living, could all be so different if they did not follow that serpent. It makes them see the tremendous influence of the people's participation in the religion of the Canaanites, an influence whose importance and gravity the people did not seem to realize. The Serpent, far from being an animal

hidden in the foliage of a tree, was the great threat which impercep-
tibly led the people to abandon the Law of God, losing themselves
in the morass of magic, losing even the meaning of human life.

It is not just a children's tale, nice perhaps for one who believes
in fables, but rather a serious taking of a stand in the face of reality,
through which the author points out clearly where lies the fault and
the root of the evils suffered by the people. It is the *Populorum
progressio* of that time.

*Would life be different if they had not followed the
Serpent?* Here a difficulty arises. The author attributes all the
evils of life to the fact that the people are listening to the voice of
the Serpent. Is this not a sign of the author's great ingenuousness?
Would the world really change if they ceased to frequent the sacred
brothels to follow more closely the Law of God? Would childbirth
then be painless, the earth without drought, religion without fear,
work without oppression?

It is not in these terms that the author poses the problem. He is
a realist, not a theoretician. He is not worried about giving an exact
idea of the total world situation; what is important for him is to
provoke some concrete transforming action. If he indicates the
root of all the world's evils, it is not because he wants to know and
teach where they all come from. He is a practical man who rather
wants to know and teach this: In the face of such a bad situation,
where should one begin so as to be able to change what is there?
Today, for example, it is relatively easy to analyze the world
situation and point to the causes of the general malaise. It is hard to
say where one should start in order to change it. The one who
succeeds in this is a genius. The author does not propound a
theory; rather he proposes a *strategy*.

At that moment the danger and the temptation to the people
were represented by the *Serpent*. At that moment in history the
building of Paradise and the elimination of all those evils of life, in
order to be effective, should begin for them with action against the
temptation of the Serpent. What mattered for the author was to
provoke such a reaction and to release a movement capable of
leading to Paradise. No other beginning was possible. For others,

living in another situation, the beginning will be different. The end will always be the same: universal peace.

However the author does not attribute all the ills of life to the fact that the people are listening to the voice of the Serpent. He does not mean to affirm that the world would know no sorrow, drought, or death if the people were to follow the Law of God. All he wants to affirm is that the starting point for man's resistance to evil in order to begin the building of a Paradise without sorrow, drought, or death must be, at that concrete moment of history, resistance to the Serpent of the Canaanite religion.

So every people should examine their own reality, finding out the nerve center to attack, launching a pluriform movement, converging from all sides, in different ways, towards the same end. This is the fidelity asked for by God. This is "to listen to these words . . . and act on them" (Matt. 7:24).

Adam and Eve: "A Man and a Woman"

Without previous preparation, the reader gets the impression that the biblical author is speaking of a very definite couple from the past to the exclusion of all others. The husband was called Adam and the wife called Eve. But this is not the case. The expression "Adam and Eve" could very well be translated "a man and a woman," since by his description of the attitude of Adam and Eve, the author wishes to characterize all those who belong to the human race. He speaks as we do when we wish to characterize a whole people. We say: "The Brazilian loves football," "The German is a worker," "The Latin American is underdeveloped." It is possible that three thousand years from now, when our present peoples and nations no longer exist, somebody will come to know of this way of speaking of ours and think that we are talking about three gentlemen, called respectively, Brazilian, German, Latin American. It will be a mistake, due to lack of knowledge.

Man tends to individualize, to concretize as much as possible what is generic and universal. This is, even today, the basis of many jokes. Nobody asks the name or address of the clergyman or the Irishman whom he has heard about in a joke. And the jokes

succeed in describing the characteristics of the clergyman; they
recount words he may have said, and they know all about his life.
This is a literary expedient that deceives nobody. Without going so
far as to say that the Paradise narrative is a joke, it does contain a
similar literary expedient.

The author is not thinking primarily of what happened histori-
cally in the past, but is thinking of what is happening around him
and maybe in him. His narrative is, as it were, a public confession.
Adam and Eve are the mirror that reflects critically the present
reality and helps to discover the fault that exists in every one of his
readers.

It is not valid to conclude from the narrative what we so often
hear: "Why do all of us have to suffer today because of a man and a
woman who died so long ago?" This would make being children of
this couple our only sin! This is not the mind of the Bible. It is
merely our deduction. It is a mistake caused by lack of knowledge.
And the error will be magnified to the extent that we try to justify
it, invoking a series of arguments that have nothing to do with the
Bible, and which merely try to make the Bible concur with our way
of thinking.

The Bible does not throw the blame onto others, but hands
back the problem and confronts man with his conscience. It wants
everyone to discover in himself the Adam and the Eve and admit:
"I am the one eating the forbidden fruit! So I am responsible for
and share responsibility in the evil that exists!" It is not a longing
lament: "It was so good in the olden days, in Paradise!" The Bible
wants people to wake up, to become conscious of the situation and
face up to the evil, to start to root out the evil within themselves
and in society.

And it is possible to conquer evil, since God continues to desire
Paradise. This firm will of God is the guarantee which the Bible
gives us with absolute certainty. Without this guarantee, the conscientization of others would be fruitless. It would be a crime,
since it would lead only to despair, revolt, and despondency.
Instead, conscientization provokes repentance, faith, courage,
positive resistance, and hope.

NOT THEORY BUT PRACTICE HAS VALUE
IN COMBATING EVIL

One of the things that impede our understanding of the Paradise narrative and the sin of Adam and Eve is our tendency to theorize about things. This tendency does not come from the Bible but from our theoretical-intellectual formation. With this mentality, we reflect on evil, seeking its causes and the meaning of its existence. Unconsciously we attribute to the author of the narrative the same mentality and preoccupation. In this we are mistaken.

In the Bible we do not have a reflection on evil, but a desire to combat evil. If there is some reflection it is with a view to the fight that must be waged. Evil is examined and analyzed, not with a theoretical but with a practical mentality, i.e., with a view to eliminating it, and with a view to the transformation or conversion of the world and of men. If the Bible points out the origin of the evil or the *original sin,* it does so not to show how the evil began, but to show how the evil may be ended. In other words, it does so in order to point out the nerve center from which a positive counterattack may be launched. Because of this intention, the root of the evil or the *original sin,* at least in the Paradise narrative, is not only nor primarily a specific event that occured at the dawn of humanity. Rather it is also and above all a lived and universal reality which takes place in the today of every generation with a dangerous and threatening power, and for which every generation is responsible, *including the first generation.*

The sin of origin, seen in this way, is concretized differently in every person, in every group, epoch, or culture. In other words, it is the principle vice, which is different in every group, in every person. Whoever wishes to eliminate the evil from within himself and attain to the good, must begin the fight by an attack on this principle vice, since there may be found the root of all the rest.

At the time that this narrative on the sin of Adam and Eve was composed, the original sin, this principal vice, was concretized in the fact that the people had left the true God to follow the serpent. A confirmation that this was the way in which evil was envisaged is found in the references made to nakedness.

THE NAKEDNESS OF ADAM AND EVE:
SEX OR SOMETHING ELSE?

The author refers twice to the nakedness of Adam and Eve, i.e., of the man and the woman (Gen. 2:25 and 3:7). Such nakedness should not be interpreted within a sexual framework, as if the author wished to characterize the sin as a sexual abuse. The references to nakedness in the two verses are, as it were, biographical details to help the reader situate what is said of the origin of evil within the life of the man and the woman, and indeed, in his own life. They help him discover within himself the weak point which ought to be attacked and which perhaps he might not see. One verse forms a bridge between the first and second parts of the narrative and the other links the second and third parts. The part recounting the sin is introduced by the reference to unperceived nakedness (Gen. 2:25), and is concluded by the reference to perceived nakedness (Gen. 3:7).

"Both the man and the woman were naked, but they were not ashamed" (Gen. 2:25). There is evoked here a concrete image of daily life, where children go naked without perceiving it and without being ashamed of their nakedness. At the start of puberty, i.e., on entering into the time of life when boys and girls began to perceive and cover their nakedness (Gen. 3:7), they were initiated into the life of the community and officially received the law that they might begin to observe it. They thus became full members of the group with all its rights and duties. They were considered adults, capable of being responsible for their actions.

The same thing that happened to all the members of the people at that time happens to the protagonists of the narrative. They are at the time of life when they pass from an unperceived to a perceived nakedness. In this way the author wishes to describe them as people beginning to be adults, capable of receiving the Law of God and of being responsible for their actions before God and the people. And indeed, like everybody else, they received the Law of God when they were given the order to eat of all the trees, including the tree of life, except the tree of knowledge of good and evil. In these two people the adult reader recognizes himself and his life.

And within him arises the question: "What will be the attitude of this man who has become an adult and who has received the Law of God as I have?"

The answer to this question is given by the author in the second part of his narrative where he describes the sin of Adam and Eve (Gen. 3:1–6). That man and that woman of Paradise do what everybody does: From the moment they receive the knowledge of the Law, there begins in them the lamentable and inexplicable transgression of it. Adam and Eve are no more and no less than a critical reflection of what was actually happening among the people but of which the people did not seem to perceive the range, importance, and gravity. Tempted, the two consent and transgress the law by listening to the voice of the Serpent. Many a reader must admit: "I am Adam" or "I am Eve!"

For the author, however, the general malaise which he notes and opposes does not come about merely because some or even many or even the whole people are falling into apostasy, detaching themselves from God. For him, this resistance to the Law of God affects not just some or many, but affects *all* in the root of their being, since he concludes: "They saw that they were naked. They put together fig leaves and made loincloths" (Gen. 3:7). He seeks to establish a link between the transgression of the Law and the perception of nakedness. Everyone is conscious of the perception of nakedness, since it is a universal human phenomenon. Not everyone is conscious of the transgression of the law of God. Most men seem to be asleep and should be awakened. The author wishes to awaken them with the allusion to nakedness. It is not his intention to explain the origin of the shame that man feels on account of his nakedness. He uses this universal phenomenon, discovered by all at the start of their adult life, to make everybody pay attention and to lead them to a serious examination of their lives: "The shame which you, man, feel on account of your nakedness is related to a fault against your God. When you came to adult age, you received the Law of God and did not observe it. You perverted your relationship with God. You are being tempted by the Serpent and perhaps have already fallen, since you wish to be your own God. Make a revision of your life and see this point."

The author does not *prove* the existence of a sin which occurred in the beginning and which would have been transmitted from father to son. He simply *notes* the existence of that mysterious and inexplicable tendency of man towards evil, when he arrives at a consciousness of himself as an adult, and when he begins to have an obligation to follow the Law of God, to take on responsibility for his acts. Inexplicably, then, he chooses evil. This is what the Bible, in other places, calls *dura cervix* (Exod. 32:9; 33:3,5; 34:9; Deut. 9:6,13; 21:27). It is the inexplicable mystery of evil which takes shape in the human heart on the very day that man begins to be free and responsible. It must be something at the root of the human being, something in him since the beginning, since birth (*cf.* Ps. 51:7; Job. 14:1–4), and which, in the author's day, was being activated and concretized by the temptation of the Serpent.

The references to nakedness are then a way of confronting the reader with the mystery of the evil which lives in him and of which he is ignorant. They do not say anything about what kind of sin it was, but serve to help man ponder over himself and recognize his fault. They seek to lead him, in that way, to a change of life that will have repercussions in all the rest of family and social life.

In this Adam, protagonist of the narrative, all the Adams, i.e., all men, recognize themselves and their lives, and perhaps awaken to their guilt and responsibility before God, before other men, before life itself. They discover the abyss of evil that lies dormant within them. This is the target at which the narrative is aiming. Only by beginning with this new awareness is it possible to open a real and valid road to the future Paradise.

Sin Changes the Relationship with God

Man's first reaction after the transgression is the awareness of guilt before God. It is not God who severed the relationship with man, since God goes looking for and calls the man (Gen. 3:9). The man noticed within himself that something had changed radically. It is he who hid himself, fleeing from the presence of God. The reason given is his perception of nakedness (Gen. 3:10). The man feels reduced to zero, since the eye of God sees through everything and reveals man to man. He is no more than a *naked man,* who feels that he is being judged by God. He feels the presence of God, no longer as a joy but as a judgment (*cf.* Gen. 3:8–11; Job 3:19–21).

Flight and fear now characterize the relationship of man with God. God is perceived as a judge who sets up an inquiry to establish responsibility (Gen. 3:11–13). And before him nobody can remain hidden, nobody can cover up the truth of his guilt. The man admits his mistake but is allowed to plead extenuating circumstances (Gen. 3:12–13). The truth is brought to light and the man admits that the root of the evil lies in the Serpent (Gen. 3:13) which awoke in him that inexplicable desire to be like God and to deny his own condition as man.

It would seem that the man sees in God a competitor (*cf.* Gen. 3:5). He wishes to conquer God and put him at his service. It is the eternal temptation of magic, which lies in wait for man whether it be in the guise of religion in the cult of the Canaanites, or in the form of secularization in the cult of modern technology. In both cases it is man who, with a broken axle, tries to fix the car of his life and establish an order that is only disorder and chaos. He should first fix the axle of his life which consists in his right relationship with God. There is no other source of peace.

DIVINE PUNISHMENT, BROUGHT ON BY HUMAN GUILT

Once guilt has been established and admitted, there comes the time for deserved punishment (Gen. 3:14–15). Here again the author does not speak as a theoretician wishing merely to give an opinion about the situation, pointing out and explaining the source of the evils of life; rather he speaks as a practical person who wishes to provoke some concrete action, beginning with the reality being lived by the people. And he envisages the transformation of that reality. It is not the origin of the evils that concerns him but the new meaning he wishes to give to those evils, interpreting them in the light of his faith in God, who wishes the well-being and the peace of men.

The situation created by the divine sentence is the real situation in which the reader has no difficulty seeing his day-to-day experience of life with all its attendant ills. Yet within the new perspective presented in the narrative by the author, this very day-to-day situation begins to make the sincere reader uncomfortable. He has to admit that his life is the opposite of what it ought to be, since it sets itself up, point by point, against the ideal situation of Paradise. He sees that if he has arrived at this point it is because he is eating the forbidden fruit, transgressing the Law of God. He sees then that this evil which is afflicting him does not exist without his being to blame, or rather that the evil will not leave the world without his collaboration. Thus, for him, the evils of life have ceased to be something natural and begin to trouble his conscience, since he feels responsible for them. He begins to look at life with different eyes.

In this way everything, even the most common phenomena of life, like the snake that crawls (Gen. 3:14), the childbirth that hurts (Gen. 3:16), the earth that does not produce (Gen. 3:18), the bread of endurance that he eats (Gen. 3:19), the death that awaits him (Gen. 3:19)—all remind him now that his life is out of joint. God no longer occupies the place he ought to because he, man, is trying to occupy the place of God (Gen. 3:5). Everything has become an appeal from God.

The author, inspired by his faith in God, was able to reveal the divine dimension in the human, a dimension that hides itself in the things of life. Everything becomes a revelation and begins to act on the conscience of the man, becoming a powerful factor in his conscientization. The action that will result in Paradise has been set in motion.

ENMITY BETWEEN THE WOMAN AND THE SERPENT

The Serpent does not get a chance to defend himself, nor could he get such a chance since he represents the force of evil, the opposite of the well-being and peace that God desires. This force, which acts in men trying to divert them from the true way of the Law of God, should be crushed. If it is not crushed, the order and peace of Paradise will never prevail.

The sentence pronounced on the Serpent has two aspects. On the one hand, it interprets certain natural phenomena in such a way as to make them a reminder of the risk man runs in the fight he must wage against evil. On the other hand, the sentence affirms that this fight is necessary, and that the final victory of good is certain.

The first aspect is this: "You will be accursed, separated from all the animals. You will have to crawl on your belly, you will have to eat the dust of the earth, forever" (Gen. 3:14). Human sensitivity sees snakes as bad, living in isolation causing disgust and, according to some, eating dust (Mic. 7:17). The fact that they crawl increases the impression that they are treacherous animals, not to be trusted. These natural phenomena are interpreted in such a way that the snake, this treacherous animal, reminds man of the danger of that other *Serpent* which tries to separate him from God. It is a popular teaching device met with even today when parents teach their children to remember God when they see, for example, the flash of lightning or when they hear the sound of thunder. It is a way of looking through reality and revealing in it the dimension of God's call. It is very real for the rural dweller, living far from civilization, constantly threatened by the danger of snakes. Maybe it does not mean as much today, but at that time it was a pedagogy perfectly adapated to the mentality of the people.

As for the second aspect, this enmity between men and snakes evokes the other enmity, between the forces of good and evil, which will be a fight to the finish. The text says: "I am going to bring about enmity between you and the woman, between your race and hers. She will crush your head and you will be able to attack her only by the heel" (Gen. 3:15). In this verse the Serpent ceased to be a simple snake, and became a symbol of the force that resists God. The woman symbolizes the human race, and in particular the people of God, insofar as it exerts itself in the struggle against evil, trying to observe and have observed the law of God.

These are the two forces that wage war throughout history. On the one hand is the man who opens himself to God, following his Law and transforming life; on the other hand is the man who closes himself within magical religion, who has ceased to believe in God and who appropriates all of life to himself, as if he himself were a god. It will be a life and death struggle. The man who follows the Serpent, eating the prohibited fruit and closing himself into his own world, is a man who dies and is the germ of death for others. The man who follows the Law of God, reacting to and resisting evil, conquers death and wins life and is the germ of life for others. At the end of history, the Serpent, i.e., that part of humanity which follows the Serpent in trying to achieve the final coup, will be crushed by the heel of the woman who generates men of faith.

In these mysterious words is expressed the unshakable faith of the Bible in the power and faithfulness with which God will bring to a conclusion his plan for order and peace. Here there appears the invincible hope with which the Bible wishes people to arm themselves in the fight against evil, aware that this fight is victorious because it is God's fight. In these words, the Bible tries to arouse all of us to a generous sharing in the effort to combat evil and build peace, knowing that any and every effort in this direction will be victorious, since it has the blessing of God.

With the progress of history and the resurrection of Christ, this still vague hope of Gen. 3:15 becomes clearer and takes on more concrete outlines for us. The woman who produces men of faith can be identified with Mary, who brought Jesus Christ into the world. Jesus is the victorious descendant of the woman, who, by his resurrection, crushed the head of the Serpent. In the resurrection of Christ, the power and fidelity of God laid the foundation stone for the definitive construction of the future Paradise. The resurrection of Christ is the perfect proof that God's plan will prevail, whatever be the contrary force of the Serpent.

The World Invaded by Evil

The description of Paradise, sin, and punishment showed that the swing to peace must begin with a reintegration of man around his true axis, God, since there, in the broken axis, lies the root of the malaise. But this will not be possible if we separate life with God from life in the world. For the Bible, the broken axis of human life brings with it the other evils of society, since the text that speaks of Paradise is united with what follows in chapters 4-11 and cannot be separated from it. What follows is merely a consequence. It is branch and fruit of the same seed. It is the result of the manifestation of the evil that is in the root and that consists in man's break with God.

It is from this point of view that chapters 4 to 11 should be read, in which the author denounces the ills that exist in society. Here too he does not confine himself to simple theory, indicating merely the origin of the evil, but rather he wishes to conscientize his contemporaries to the responsibility of each for the transformation of this abnormal state of humanity and for the restoration of order and peace in the world.

The evils of society can be studied and analyzed from different angles: economic, sociological, philosophic, ethnic, political. The Bible, however, regards them from the point of view of faith and hope in God.

In Paradise man cut himself off from God. Cut off from God and closed into himself, man no longer perceives the meaning of the other in his life. He shuts himself completely into his egoism, which culminates in the death of Abel. Death makes its entry into the world. Cain who kills his brother is everyone who kills another. Cain is the mirror denouncing each and every act of assassination as contrary to God, and as an inevitable consequence of the break with God. The frequent question of "Whom did Cain marry—his sister?" has no meaning within this perspective. The question is *ours* and would not be possible within the mentality of the Bible, since there were thousands of Cains living in the author's day, and even today many of them are roaming free throughout the world.

Cut off from God and cut off from the other, man takes up a defensive position which generates violence. Violence increases at an alarming rate, since violence begets violence and control is no longer possible. And so Lamech cries out: "Sevenfold vengeance is taken for Cain, but seventy-sevenfold for Lamech" (Gen. 4:24). This was the image of the relationship between the peoples and tribes of the author's time. It has not changed much since.

Cut off from God, cut off from each other, living in a climate of violence, threats, and insecurity, man feels lost, without protection or help. In desperation he seeks salvation in the domain of rite and magic to the point of utterly confusing divine and human (Gen. 6:1–4), and of corrupting the meaning of life (Gen. 6:7). Man can deliberately endanger the order and the survival of his race.

The Bible interprets in this way the natural disasters which break the regular rhythm of nature and life. They should not be

seen as blind forces brought about by the arbitrary will of the
divinities, thus justifying the alienation of men into the magic rites
of superstitious cult. The author presents these disasters in such a
way as to make their meaning clear and reveal in them an appeal of
God to the conscience of man.

It is for science to investigate whether or not the flood was
historical. If science should decide it was, one should not say,
"See! The Bible was right!" The Bible is not interested in being
"right" on this point. It is interested in being right on another
point, i.e., that magic is one of the worst evils afflicting man. What
would be the advantage of proving that the flood was historical as
long as nature with all its dangers and disasters remains a closed
book which continues to provoke an appeal to magic as the response of timid and threatened man?

Finally, if man continues in this direction of isolation from God
and from others in which he protects himself against threats by
violence, vengeance, and magic, then he ends in total disintegration, in a confusion that prevents any action in common. This is the
confusion symbolized by the dispersal of the people which resulted
from the building of the tower of Babel (Gen. 11:7–9).

This is the vision that the Bible offers of the world's invasion by
evil. Evil enters through a narrow, almost invisible crack, through
a tiny seed, but goes on spreading and growing until it reaches the
immensity of the ills noted and opposed by the author. To discuss
original sin and forget or fail to see the evils which today afflict
people is a contradiction. To discuss whether original sin is transmitted by heredity or some other way while *not* recognizing the
calls of God which summon our consciences on the basis of the
evils stamped on people all around us is the type of alienation
which contradicts the vision of things offered by the Bible.

THE TIME FACTOR

In the Bible, the causality of evil is not understood solely in terms
of time. That is, the author does not see the origin of evil or original
sin as a cause, put in motion in the distant past and still acting on
the present through a relationship of cause and effect. He sees it
rather as a present cause, put in motion at every moment by the

free actions of man. For him, original sin not only happened—it is happening all the time, since the beginning. It is not just a fact pertaining to the past but a living wound that stays with men along the way of life, ceaselessly causing blood to flow. It is that mysterious and very active tendency in man towards evil which man manifests, takes on, and increases by his free decisions, thus contributing to the evils already existing around him. In this way, the Bible reveals that nobody can wash his hands before the evils of life and society, and exclusively take the role of accuser of humanity without any need to place himself in the ranks of the guilty.

Original sin is like a snowslide that crashes down from the top of a mountain and in its fall destroys the village on the plain. The end result of original sin is not the expulsion from Paradise, but rather the universal disintegration of humanity, evidenced by the tower of Babel. And this force must be understood, not just as rolling through the ages, but also and above all, as one that is crashing down at every moment within man, and at every moment is destroying villages.

We all have a share of blame, since in each of us there is an Adam who eats of the forbidden fruit. Because of this, in each of us there lies dormant a Cain, capable of killing his brother. In each of us there can arise a Lamech, to spread violence and vengeance without limit. All of us can bring on a deluge of disintegration when we interfere unduly with God's world, and when we transform religion into a mere rite and a faithless, lifeless, magic ceremony. All of us build the tower of Babel and cause confusion when we seek to dominate by dividing and causing separation.

Personal evil and social evil, personal reform and social reform.   It is in this way that the Bible, in the first eleven chapters of Genesis, presents and opposes the evils of the world. There is a close connection between personal evil and collective evil. At the root of social evils lies the personal sin of man's break with God. If there is evil in the world it is because man does not put himself in his rightful place before the Creator. In other words, it would not help nor would it be possible to fight against the confusion of the tower of Babel, against the disintegration that caused the flood, against murderous violence, without trying at the same time once more to join man to his Creator, by convincing him that he should not eat of the forbidden fruit. Neither would it be right to let him be crushed by the evils of the world around him and lose himself in lamentations, worrying only about his own private life: "Patience! I cannot do a thing, nor am I to blame for all this!"

It might seem madness for somebody to try to react against the evils of the world by starting with a sincere reform of his own life. Humanly speaking, it would be an inefficient act, giving no result. But it is precisely in this that the Bible believes, since God is the one who guarantees it. Just as there is a link between personal evil and social evil, there is also a link between personal and family reform and socio-collective reform.

The Bible does not believe in a social reform that does not have personal reform as its base. Such a reform will have no future, will not lead to Paradise. Neither does it believe in a purely personal reform, cut off from social life. That would be ineffectual. One cannot put himself in his rightful place before God without taking into consideration the place of the individual in society. On the other hand, neither is is possible to put oneself in his rightful position before God without taking into consideration society as made up of free people, each of whom has his own personal destiny.

An Expedition in Search of Paradise

To become aware of evil is a shattering experience. Things that seemed to be the result of blind forces for which man seemed to be in no way to blame and on which he seemed to have no influence appear now in another light. They are presented as being exclusively the responsibility of man. Man, looking at his condition of misery and abandonment and oppression, no longer has the right to appeal to God, asking for help as if the situation depended on God alone and not on man. In the Paradise narrative he has seen and noted that the final cause of all is within man himself. And this cause did not merely, nor primarily occur in some long distant past, but also and above all it is in a very real sense present and continuous: "I, now, am to blame for this." Men should be aware of this. If they are surrounded by evil, they should not attribute this to any outside interference, whether it be of gods or other mysterious forces, but solely to themselves as they live today, joined together for good or ill.

The one responsible for all is man. He should not, however, rebel against evil. He should take upon himself the situation as it is, accept it as one accepts a punishment, and fight to put an end to evil. He has the power to do this, since God wants him to fight evil by building peace. This is his mission. And in this perspective, every prayer has meaning and efficacy.

The Bible expresses this when it says that Paradise was not destroyed but continues to exist. God merely put an angel at the entrance to prevent an improper approach by man (Gen. 3:22–24). Such an improper approach would be any attempt by man to take possession of life forever, without reconsidering his position as one who had broken with God. In affirming that Paradise continues to exist, the Bible is not seeking to affirm that in some part of the world, in some undiscovered place, there is a wonderful but inaccessible garden. This garden, as garden, never existed and does not exist.

What existed and continues to exist is the real and always open possibility of man's ability to realize, with God's support, that universal peace symbolized by the garden. The only expedition that will be able to find the earthly Paradise is the one that sets out for the future, letting itself be guided by the Law of God, which now is the Law of Christ. Only in that direction can man find life.

In the present situation, disintegration is already a fact. Merely to seek immortality while leaving the rest undone, without setting things right, just won't do. A car on the highway goes fast and soon reaches its destination. If the car is stuck in the mud by the roadside, it is of little avail to leave the car and proceed on foot along the highway. Car and all should arrive at the destination. And in this case the effort to arrive becomes more painful and difficult. Humanity is like a car stuck in the mud by the roadside. Many do not notice this and make it sink even deeper into the mud, making the task of extricating it more difficult. If the car got stuck, it was because of carelessness—the highway is not to blame. Nonetheless, the duty of arriving at the destination still remains. Now the cross is driven into the middle of the highway. No use trying to bypass it. It is the way which leads to the end, which is the peace of the resurrection. There is no other way. This is what it means to be a realist and to look at reality with the eyes of faith.

Jesus Christ took this road and reached the end. He let it be known that our broken-down expedition to Paradise should not lose heart. The car can be pulled from the mud of the roadside and put once more on the highway that leads to our destination.

God walks with man, man must walk with God. God did not abandon man, but keeps on protecting him, even after his sin. God did not break off the relationship. Because of this, even in the face of crushing reality, man cannot create in himself a feeling of despair. He must be an optimist. The Bible expresses this certainty of the good will of God when it says that he made clothes for Adam and Eve immediately after he had inflicted the punishment of their sin (Gen. 3:20). God helps man to cover his nakedness. This means that through the relationship he maintains with man, the latter awakes to a realization of his own worth and grows as a man, escaping from his nothingness and casting off his feeling of guilt. God protects Cain after he has expelled him from the country (Gen. 4:14–15). He saves the human race from the flood by saving Noah from the waters (Gen. 6:8; 7:1; 9:19). In the end when the confusion caused by building the tower of Babel made impossible any joint action by all mankind, God calls Abraham so that with him he might reach once more *all* the peoples of the earth: "*All* the families of the earth will be blessed in you" (Gen. 12:3).

With Abraham there begins what we are accustomed to call the history of salvation. It is the reply of God's fidelity to man, who feels powerless before the reality that crushes him. The alliance of God with man already began in the creation and was renewed with Noah (Gen. 9:8–17). It is in order to bring about this alliance, made with all men, that God now makes an alliance with the particular group of Abraham. In this way, the Bible places the people of God within the setting of the human race and clarifies the mission it is destined to realize: to help redirect men into the way of life that leads to Paradise, or rather, redirect man into the building of peace. In this way it is made clear that God walks with men. Man can only walk well if he decides to keep in step with God.

Here one should not apply only criteria of time, as if there were first a natural phase from Adam to Abraham; then the phase of the Law of Moses, from the beginning of the history of salvation until Jesus Christ; finally, the third and last phase in which we live today, characterized by the law of Jesus Christ. Here too —especially here—we are dealing with phases or epochs that are contemporaneous. In ever epoch of history, right up to today, there are people living like Adam, like Cain, like Lamech, like those who provoked the deluge, like those who built the tower of Babel. In every epoch there are people who live like Abraham and like the Hebrew people. And since Christ came, there are people who live according to the Gospel. These are not successive phases of history, one excluding the other. They are different levels of awareness, existing at the same time in humanity and even with people, faced with the evils that afflict man.

The function of the group that decides to walk with God. The group that comes into existence with the calling of Abraham is, as it were, God's party in the world. It is the people of God, which walks with God, since it believes in the possibility of eliminating evil by the power of God, of bringing about a transformation, and of building Paradise in complete harmony, realizing in this way the aim of the Creator.

This people is aware of the problem in its very depths, since its awareness springs, not from the false root, noted and opposed in Adam and Eve, but from the true root which is life with God (*cf.* Gen. 17:1–2), later to be outlined and made official in the alliance. The alliance with God implies an agreement to observe the Law of God (*cf.* Exod. 24:3–8) which becomes the norm of its life and action. Thus they refused to eat of the tree of knowledge of good and evil. In this group, conflict between brothers is being eliminated, murder is prohibited, and love of neighbor is a duty (Lev. 19:18). Cain is no longer permitted to kill Abel. Having a true relationship with God, based on faith, in trust and friendship, they condemn every kind of empty ritualism and magic that would lead to the flood (*cf.* Exod. 20:1–17). For them, the only approach to

God is by the entrance of faith. They want to be a group that exists in order to serve and to help, not to dominate or to protect its own interests. They do not close themselves in on their own privileges, regarding themselves as better or stronger than others, but seek to be "a kingdom of priests and a consecrated nation" (Exod. 19:6), a definition that expresses an attitude of service, the opposite of that which led to the confusion of Babel. By acting thus, they place themselves on the road that leads to Paradise.

With the coming of Jesus Christ, God's project took shape, and in fact Paradise became a reality in the resurrection. Because of this, St. Paul regards the risen Jesus as a "new Adam" (*cf.* Rom. 5:12–19). And St. John, in the Book of Revelation, describes the future awaiting us with images drawn from Paradise. "There will be no more death, and no more mourning or sadness. The world of the past is gone" (Rev. 21:4). Nothing unclean may come into it [the city] . . . the angel showed me the river of life . . . flowing crystal clear down the middle of the city street. On the other side of the river were the trees of life, which bear twelve crops of fruit in a year, one in each month, and the leaves of which are the cure for the pagans. (Rev. 21:27–22:2). It is Paradise, realized at last. All men will be God's people (Rev. 21:3). Everything there will be new (Rev. 21:5). There will be a new heaven and a new earth and God will be all in all (Rev. 21:1; 1 Cor. 15:28), like a lamp that scatters its light into the most hidden corners (Rev. 22:5). It will be the total resurrection, which began with Abraham, of which we got a sample in Jesus Christ, and which will be brought to completion in the last time. It will really be life, abundance of life (John 10:10), life eternal that will never end. It will be immortality, communicated by divine wisdom, born directly of God.

The Church, the group raised up by God, must serve as an instrument in the realization of all this. It must be a more aware group, a group that knows the meaning of life and carries it forward, resisting and transforming, never wearying, opening a path throughout the dense jungle of the world's ills, moving towards Paradise.

CHAPTER FIVE

Responding to the Difficulties and Problems

Now that we have finished our interpretation, we must turn to the difficulties and problems that we raised at the start. Many questions have already been answered. Others, however, need to be discussed in greater depth. New questions arose as we outlined our interpretation. Both will be discussed in this chapter. Discussing them can help us to see with greater clarity what was said up to now, and free us from certain restraints that may have impeded the action of the Word of God in our lives.

The Man Made from Clay and the Woman Formed from the Rib of the Man

The image or simile of God the Potter is frequent in the Bible. The prophet Jeremiah wrote: "As the clay is in the potter's hand, so are you in mine, says the Lord" (Jer. 18:6; *cf.* Isa. 29:15–16; 45:9–13; 64:8). Here, nothing is said about the way in which man was created. All that is done is to trace the characteristics of an existential and permanent condition of human life, by calling attention to its radical dependence and extreme fragility. Man does not have his destiny in his hands. His life is in the hands of God like clay in the hands of the potter. It *breaks* very easily.

The author of the Paradise narrative made use of this well-known image to show that the first duty of man is to accept himself as he is, in his condition as a creature before God. In this lies the beginning of true wisdom (*cf.* Ecclus. 1:16,20). There is no use revolting against this. It would be like the tree revolting against being wood. However, the way in which the author used the image is different. Instead of staying on the literary plane of simple comparison, as did the prophet Jeremiah, he concretized the image and presented God in the role of potter, modeling the man.

The same is true of the forming of the woman from the rib of the man. God literally made real a popular saying: "Bone of my bones, flesh of my flesh" (Gen. 2:23). It is as if in trying to concretize the slang expression "Go jump in a lake" someone were to paint a man jumping into a lake. Anybody who knows the language would not be deceived by such a painting and would get the message of the painter: "Get out of my sight as fast as you can!" Thus, in a simple, popular way the author lets it be known that one should respect the mysterious attraction of the sexes and the unity of marriage in which man and woman mutually complete one another. This has to do with God.

The deep sleep into which God caused Adam to fall does not refer to an anesthetic to make the operation less painful. They had little knowledge of surgery. It has to do with their concept of the creative action. To create is God's secret. Only he knows the secret and only he knows how to do it (cf. Ps. 139:13–15; 2 Mac. 7:22). Man cannot witness it. Because of this, he sleeps while God creates.

The Bible, however, says nothing concrete about the way in which the man was created or how the woman came to be. It is dealing with the human problem of the author's day. It wishes to give the vision of faith about things. The decision concerning the viability of the hypotheses on evolution, on monogenism or polygenism, belongs to science, not to the Bible. The Bible says nothing about them. Neither for nor against. If people have difficulties of faith about these matters, these do not come from the Bible but from the traditional way of interpreting the Bible. We have not yet succeeded in separating revealed truth from the mind-set with which we envisage and interpret such truth. Whoever wishes to question the hypotheses of science should not invoke the Bible, except when science tries to offer an all-encompassing vision of man that excludes or contradicts the vision of faith which the Bible gives us about life and history. And even then, the theologian should be very careful not to confuse his own mind-set with revealed truth.

This, however, does not mean that the exegete can interpret the Bible without taking into consideration all these problems which are being debated in the Church. If he explains the Bible, he explains it not up in the air, but for real people, living in the midst of the problems of life and conditioned by them. It would be of little use to launch a new idea if there were nobody to accept it. Such an idea resembles a man-made satellite returning from the moon. If it does not reach the narrow corridor of entry into the earth's atmosphere, it will pass by the earth and lose itself in the immensity of space.

- This explanation clarifies, too, the apparent contradiction in the Bible which in one place says that man was the first to be created, in another that he was the last. These are two different ways of describing the place of man in the world. Today we do the same thing. At times the last person in the line is the most important; at other times, the first. It depends on the point of view and the ceremonial.

Were the Names of the First Couple "Adam" and "Eve"?

What were the names of the first couple? The answer is Adam and Eve. We take it then that these two names were proper names like John and Mary. We think of a specific couple.

We have already seen that the Bible does not think along these lines. It does not even set out to speak solely of the first couple. What it sets out to speak of is the whole of humanity, represented and personified in the two protagonists of the narrative, called simply Man and Woman, or Adam and Issha. The name *Eve* appears only at the end, after the sin (Gen. 3:20). Eve is a symbolic name that indicates the role of the woman: to be a mother.

So Adam and Eve did not exist?. They did exist, they do exist, they will exist, since they are all of us, our ancestors, back to the first couple, ourselves, our children and grandchildren, down to the last one to exist on the face of the earth.

So there was no first couple? There was, since we exist. Without a first couple, there could never have been a second. What we do not know is the name of this first couple. We only know that they were human persons, *adam* and *issha*, men and women, and that there existed in them what exists in all of us, i.e., that mysterious and inexplicable tendency to evil. How did this come about? We do not know, and the Bible does not tell us. After all, it is of little interest. The Bible speaks of the Adam who lived at the time that it was written. And today we must think, not so much of the Adam of the beginning, but of the Adam who lives in all of us.

Would the World and Life Be Different If There Had Been No Sin?

According to the Bible, if Adam and Eve had not sinned the earth would be without deserts, life without death, childbirth without pain, love without oppression; the animals would be gentle, the serpent would not crawl. How can the Bible make such things depend on human failure since, in most cases, these are natural phenomena in which the free action of man is not involved? They had already existed long before man appeared on the face of the earth.

The reply to this question has already been given in part. The question is badly put. It presupposes that the Bible is speaking of a single, definite couple, and that it intends, in some way, to throw on this couple the blame for the evils that exist. It presupposes that the narrative is giving concrete information about the historical origin of things. But the author does not speak here of facts of the past, nor does he try to give scientific theories about the historical origin of the present situation. What he speaks of is future possibilities which man loses by his bad conduct. If he speaks of origins, he does so to call attention to that point or that root from which the counterattack should be launched, since it is there that evil enters into life, obstructing the future which God has in store for man. To speak of origins to explain the present is a very frequently used device in the Bible called *etiology*.

Nobody knows how the world would be if man had never sinned. Nobody can say how the world will be when man has ceased to do evil and is completely integrated with God, his Creator. This escapes any kind of observation or research. Not even the Bible knows, nor does it mean to give concrete information about such a topic. It is true that the Bible says a lot about the future of peace that awaits us. But it presents it in a language drawn from life and from human history. Moments of intense happiness and joy are projected on the screen of the future to give us some idea of what we can expect. Jesus Christ, for example, compares this future to a wedding feast (Matt. 22:1–10) and to a banquet (Matt. 22:4). He speaks of the house of the Father (John 14:2), of a feast (Luke 14:24), and of so many other images and realities of life, to indicate that very future. But all of this is symbolic language. Beginning with the things we know, it suggests an immense happiness, a full realization of man and a full and integral peace that outstrips all our thought categories. "No eye has seen and no ear has heard . . . all that God has prepared for those who love him" (1 Cor. 2:9).

The faith and hope expressed in this symbolic language leaps over every possible and impossible barrier. The criterion they use in imagining the future is not our reality with its natural possibilities, but rather the unlimited power of God, who placed himself on the side of man, to be one with him.

This is also true of the description of Paradise where things are spoken of which, humanly speaking, are impossible, even absurd: land without drought, childbirth without pain, life without death, love without oppression, gentle animals that speak, religion without fear. In this narrative the Bible goes beyond limits never passed in real life. The reason for this is that the author believes in a future that surpasses anything man can imagine, in a future to be created by the unlimited and unimaginable power of the goodness of God, the realization of which will depend on the free collaboration of man. The evils of the world and of life are interpreted as being in culpable contrast with this future. They accuse man. He is not collaborating.

Within this perspective, the evils thus interpreted take on a double significance or symbolism. On the one hand, they remind man: "You are responsible for the evils you suffer. It is in your power to build your own happiness." On the other hand, they remind man of his limits: "The crowning point of your happiness must come from another, from God. Paradise is locked and only God has the key. With your own strength you cannot open it; just look at what you succeed in doing with all your attempts to remedy these evils and restore order. The disorder has become worse!"

God opened the door of Paradise only once up to now. That was in the resurrection of Jesus Christ. And that one time fully jusitifies the hope expressed in the description of Paradise.

Consequently, the description of Paradise is valuable as an ideal capable of catalyzing our efforts and of arousing new hope and energy for action.

In the same way we can explain the problem of the spring that rises in Paradise and then divides into four great rivers, the four greatest of that time. Had the author lived in our day, he might have spoken of the Volga of Russia, the Rhine of Europe, the Mississippi of North America, and the Amazon of South America. The geographic location of Paradise, situated in the place where the Nile, Ganges, Tigres, and Euphrates rise, shows clearly that the author is not thinking of a real orchard, situated in some part of the globe. He merely imagines an ideal situation, in which the abundance of water to combat drought exceeds anything known to man on earth. Only God himself succeeds in bringing about such a "new earth" (Isa. 66:22).

In this context we can explain the image of the cherubim who stand guard at the entrance to Paradise to prevent any undue approach by man (Gen. 3:24). It is an image from Babylonian mythology, which speaks of *karibu*, a hybrid animal, part man, part lion, part eagle, part bull. It represented an extremely strong being, stronger than the powers of man. The meaning of this symbolism is as follows: Man, by himself, is radically incapable of building his own happiness: it is beyond his real ability. The power needed to realize this aim will come to life in man the moment he links up again with the Creator, through his observance of the Law of God. An act of faith in the power and faithfulness of God must lie at the root of every human effort. If not, man's efforts are doomed to perish in the karibus of his own myths and the tree of life will remain inaccessible forever.

To Beget Many Sons in the Pains of Childbirth

Many think that the modern technique of painless childbirth may not be used, since the Bible says: "It is with pains that you will bring forth your children" (Gen. 3:16). Those who apply this technique would be going against God, since they would not be submitting to the punishment that lies upon us all.

In fact, this statement does occur in the Bible. But I believe we interpret it badly. The pain of childbirth is a reality. It exists. The Bible merely wishes to interpret this real life fact, and link it to God's call to conversion. We do the same thing today. Do not many people see a call from God in an escape from a disaster? Thus, the pain of childbirth should remind woman that her situation in the world is affected by a deep evil which may be cured if she turns to God. The Bible, as we have already seen in other places, wishes to make reality transparent, since it is convinced that human life, with all its motives for laughter and tears, is overflowing with moments of revelation that pass by unperceived.

Thus the very effort being made today to lessen and eliminate the pains of childbirth should remind man of his obligation to make a similar effort to link up his life anew with God. The same is true of our efforts to make the land more fertile, to domesticate the animals, to abolish illness and sorrow, to eliminate injustice and disorder, to improve working conditions, to normalize the relationships of human love. All these efforts should cease to be neutral and must become an appeal to people's conscience, calling them to make a similar effort within themselves by being converted to the Creator. Thus our reality and even our technology, so empty of God and of spiritual values, can acquire once more their symbolic value without losing their autonomy. This could contribute efficaciously to the growth of the spirit, so underdeveloped in this age of development.

Pope Pius XII stimulated research on the techniques of painless childbirth when he said that the Bible says nothing against it. Some exegetes tried to prove the Pope's statement by making a detailed analysis of the Hebrew word translated as *pain*. They arrived at the conclusion that the meaning of the Hebrew word is wider and includes worries, preoccupations, cares, disillusion, deceptions, sacrifices, sufferings, pains. I do not know if such reasoning is correct. I believe that the author of the narrative was really thinking of the *pains of childbirth*, since this is the most common meaning of the Hebrew word. But the author does not mean to say that childbirth *must* be accompanied by pains. He merely states a fact. In reality, childbirth was accompanied by many pains. His message is this: Let these pains remind man of his situation of rupture with God and spur him on to a sincere conversion.

For the biblical author, the begetting of children is seen as a way to overcome the death that afflicts men. In Paradise there will be neither procreation nor childbirth, since there will be no death. By means of procreation, man and woman prolong their lives in their children. By her painful childbirth, the woman contributes to the building of Paradise, since one day her descendant will crush the head of the Serpent. St. Paul compares this long history of life, which is constantly being reborn and seeking happiness, to a long and arduous pregnancy which is coming to an end (Rom. 8:22). Here, perhaps, the Bible has something critical to say of our present individualism and personalism. It makes relative the pretensions of those whose horizons end with the personal interests of their own human realization. It calls attention to the fact that we are all part of a long line of generations, one following on the other. The individual destiny of each person will depend on the general destiny of all. The destiny of each person will be reached and realized to the extent that he has made his contribution to the realization of that destiny of all. It is within this perspective that the Bible sees the role of the woman, called to be a mother.

Was the Talking Serpent the Devil?

The Serpent spoke. Animals do not speak. How can we explain this? Maybe it is not an apt comparison but the person who today reads "Donald Duck" is not surprised at a duck speaking like a man. In *The Little Prince* the animals speak. In fables the animals speak. Nobody complains or objects. The same is true of the Paradise narrative.

Was the Serpent which spoke the devil? This interpretation of the figure of the Serpent was given in the Book of Wisdom: "It was the devil's envy that brought death into the world" (Wisd. 2:24). Later still, in the Book of Revelation, it is stated: "The great dragon, the primeval Serpent, known as the devil or Satan, who had deceived all the world, was hurled down" (Rev. 12:9). In these two passages the identification between Serpent and devil is already a fact. How did this happen?

As we have seen, the Serpent was the symbol of the Canaanite religion, which led the people away from the Law of God. Because of this, it became the symbol of the force contrary to God, which concretized itself in different ways in the different epochs of history. Thus it came about that the image of the Serpent, little by little, moved away from its initial symbolism as the sign of the Canaanite religion to become simply the symbol of evil. In the Book of Wisdom an attempt is made to individualize this power of evil and the name "devil" is given to it. Thus the words *Serpent, devil,* and *Satan* became synonyms indicating the power that opposes God and tries to turn people away from the right path.

For the author of the Revelation, the Serpent, which had by now taken on the proportions of "an enormous dragon" (Rev. 12:9), was concretized and incarnated in the Roman Empire (*cf.* Rev. 13:1–10), since it was to this empire, symbolized by the beast, that the dragon gave his powers.

The fundamental question we are left with is: In what form is this diabolic force incarnated today, opposing God and leading men astray?

Why Didn't God Give Adam and Eve Another Chance?

This question, too, presupposes that the Bible is speaking of a definite, historical couple at the beginning of the history of mankind. This is not the case.

Besides, this kind of question leads the problem off center. It transfers the problem to God and to that representative couple: to God, because he did not give man another chance; to the couple, because they did not get such a chance. And we spend time discussing the motives God might have had for refusing them such a chance. The real problem, however, is not God's nor Adam and Eve's, but ours. God, in fact, is giving all of us such an opportunity at every instant, ever since the time of the *first* couple or the first couples, until today. He is giving this opportunity to the Adam and Eve that lives in each of us. And he will continue to give the same opportunity as long as there are people left on earth. If we are displeased with the condition of the world, we should not transfer this problem by asking: "Why didn't God give that couple another chance?"; rather we should look into our own conscience and ask: "Why are we not accepting, not even perceiving the opportunity which God is giving us and which is always at our disposal?"

So the real problem is ours, since it depends on us whether the world will continue in its ambiguity and violence or will be transformed into a dwelling place worthy of man, called by God to intimacy with him. To become aware of this responsibility and to take it seriously might lead us onto paths we would prefer not to follow. Any excuse for alienation or transferal is welcome then, since it puts our consciences to sleep, no matter how much we may think that we are an awakened people. Thus, many of the questions we pose are perhaps subsconsious efforts to keep our consciences from waking up.

What Kind of Sin Did Adam and Eve Commit?

The question would be better formulated and would be more in accord with the objective of the Bible in the following form: "What kind of sin is being committed today by Adam and Eve?" And the answer to this question cannot come from a simple rationalized deduction, based exclusively on the exegesis of Genesis 2:4–3:24. Just as the author of Genesis 2:4–3:24 found a satisfactory reply for his time by starting with a careful analysis of reality made in the light of his faith in God, so we today must find our own reply. It is not enough to know the intellectual content of faith, since faith will only let us see its true content and call when it is related to our reality. If our attitude in the face of reality is one of omission or alienation, we close the only window we have on the landscape of faith, and we will never come to understand the full importance of faith in God for life. Two wires are needed to light a bulb. Two things are needed to light in us the lamp of faith: the Word of God and the reality of life. Our greatest defect today is not the lack of reflection on the things of faith, contained in the Word of God; rather it is our lack of knowledge of reality and the lack of reflection on this reality, made in the light of the Word of God. And when we say reflection, we do not mean the platonic meditation of one who is not involved, but a practical reflection with a view to conversion and tranformation.

The question of the kind of sin Adam and Eve committed has already caused much ink to flow. But it is a futile question to which there is no reply. First, the question is badly put. It presupposes that the Bible is talking about what happened at the beginning of the history of humanity. But nobody knows anything about this, and the Bible neither gives nor tries to give concrete information. Second, this question transfers an urgent problem—to be resolved by each person in his own life and by all of us in our lives as a group—into the field of historical and theoretical discussion which has no influence on the life of today. Third, the author wanted to give information about what was happening around him and maybe within him. His narrative, instead of being a history book, is rather a public confession of sin intended to provoke in the rest of us the same awareness of and repentance for evil.

Does that mean that nothing is said of the sin of the first man? Quite the contrary! It says as much about that sin as it does about our own: that at the root of every evil there is man's break with his Origin who is God. But nothing is said about the exact way in which that abuse of liberty by man before God was made concrete at the beginning of human history; just as nothing is said about the exact way in which the same abuse of liberty before God is being made concrete in us today. The Bible merely gives the information that this abuse of liberty at a specific time, i.e., precisely at the time of the writing of the narrative, was being made concrete in the apostasy of the people, who turned from the Law of God by preferring the magic fertility cult of the Canaanites.

As in the time of the author of the narrative, so today the great sin of Adam, this fundamental rupture of man with God, is hidden. People do not perceive it. They do not perceive the root which should be attacked in order to be able to open a road leading to the peace of Paradise. We are asleep. We are unaware. We do not react anymore. We are being massified into a total ignorance with regard to the true gravity of our situation before God, and for that very reason, of our situation before ourselves, before others, and before nature. We perceive that something must be wrong, but we do not know just what. There is even an attempt to justify, in the name of God, this condition of somnolence: we use God as a drug, as an anesthetic, as a narcotic so that man does not wake up. Racism is defended by some in the name of faith. A people is dominated by another in the name of Christian civilization. And the remedy is worse than the disease. The aim is to make all things new (Rev. 21:5). But to make new without taking into account the demands of God, to try to force an entry into a possible earthly Paradise without beginning with faith in the power and fidelity of God, is to come up against the cherubim who guard the entrance. It is because of this that today Cain runs wild and nobody can restrain him. Violence, terrorism, torture, and vengeful repression increase without control; magic, be it religious or secularized, tears everything apart and provokes a deluge. The final result is a divided and confused humanity, which fails to come to any agreement in spite of conferences for peace, just as the tower of Babel was the final result in the time of the author.

In the light of all this, there is no point in engaging in an academic discussion about the kind of sin committed by Adam and Eve. We would resemble those who "strain out gnats and swallow camels" (Matt. 23:24). We would be like a man who does not know how to educate his children, whose marriage has given only criminals to society, but who nevertheless has the affrontery to charge his neighbor with the fact that his children do not wash their hands before meals.

Original sin is stamped on humanity like a terrible wound. To ignore it is possible only by inventing another sin with the same name. What must be done is what the author tried to do in the face of reality: to try to convince men that the hidden root, the sin of origin of all this, is the break with God. It is easy to affirm this truth as a theory. What is hard is knowing how to show present reality in such a way that it becomes an appeal of God to the conscience of men, a call to review their position and be reconciled with the Creator. The biblical author realized this objective for the reality of his time. We have not yet realized it for the reality of our time. Here is one of the challenges that the Bible gives to us. Today's Abraham awaits the call: "Leave your land." If the call does not come, let us not blame Abraham or God, but ourselves. The faith and hope that animate us do not appear clearly enough in our lives.

The State of Happiness and Justice Lost by Adam

We are dealing here with the so-called "supernatural and preternatural gifts" which characterized the condition of the first man in Paradise. We are used to saying that Adam, because of his sin, lost the gifts of justice, integrity, and immortality: that he lost happiness too and became subject to concupiscence; that we are all suffering today because of him.

But to think in this way would be to give a false interpretation of the text of the Bible. It would distort the meaning of the supernatural and preternatural gifts. They are real gifts. Nobody denies them, even though some theologians and preachers have given a rather exaggerated description of this lost happiness. Maybe they did so in order to awaken the conscience of Christians. We doubt if they succeeded. They stirred up nostalgia rather than the hope of "a new heaven and a new earth" (Rev. 21:1).

We should not state the problem of the gifts in terms of the past. That is, we should not present things as if Adam had lost for all of us that happiness for which we were created. *We* are Adam and Eve. *We* are the ones who are losing those gifts at every instant. But we can regain them at every instant. What is at stake is not so much an initial or experimental state from which man fell, losing himself later in the primitivism evidenced by archeology and paleontology. It is rather that real possibility which God opened and still opens on the future horizon of human existence. Paradise is a prophecy of the future projected into the past. God confirmed the certainty we have of this future of ours by the resurrection of

Jesus Christ. In the resurrection of Jesus Christ, the future of man
is fully realized: justice, immortality, integrity, happiness, absence
of all evils.

The loss of the supernatural and preternatural gifts should not
be regarded as a fall from a state which previously existed. Rather
it is the free and responsible fall of all of us when we turn away from
the path that leads to that future state of peace and happiness,
described as Paradise and confirmed, in anticipation, by the resurrection.

At every moment, man can place himself on this path or withdraw from it. He can open before himself this future guaranteed by
God or he can close it. It is like what everyone experiences in life.
At every moment there is opened before me the possibility of
realizing myself as a human person. Whether this possibility will
be realized or not depends on my free choice. But by accepting and
taking on such a possibility I am not already realized. It is a slow
and painful growth, which becomes ever more difficult the more I
am unfaithful to this destiny of mine.

By this we do not mean to say that original sin is a simple
defect, inherent in all growth. It is not the imperfection of the one
who has not yet reached the ideal. It is not the same as calling the
child imperfect when compared with the adult it should one day
become. Such a manner of speaking does not seem correct, nor
does it correspond to the meaning of the biblical text. It would
eliminate the aspect of blame and responsibility, so strongly stressed by the Bible, since a child is not to blame for being a child and
for having the defects proper to childhood. At best, this way of
explaining original sin is no more than a new attempt at har-
monism, that is, at trying to get science to agree with the data of
faith without changing the old framework in which faith remains
imprisoned. This approach continues to try to confine to the past
the cause of the evils we suffer today; it finds a new and acceptable
formula in the defects inherent in every growing thing. In reality,
however, this explanation combines science and faith to the detri-
ment of both.

What the Bible is dealing with is the real, true blame that
belongs to every one of us for the evils that exist around us. It

wants to get us to look at this world realistically and discover in it the exact point at which we today are either contributing to the increase of evil, by turning away from the road which leads to Paradise, or are reacting against this evil, by building the happiness exemplified by the supernatural and preternatural gifts.

Where Did the Author Get His Information?

Everything indicates that the author did not consult any historical archive to get his information about the events he narrates. Nor was there any need to do so, since he intended to describe what was happening all around him. He merely used the language known at that time. He drew everything from the common core of culture of the peoples of the ancient Middle East.

In all of this, however, he was inspired by God. It is our belief that in all his work of analyzing reality and describing it as he did, the author was being guided by God. For this reason what he produced should be attributed to God. It is God who desires to communicate the message which the author communicates, and it is God who wishes to produce the awakening of conscience which the author is aiming at. God, who became man in Jesus Christ, assuming equality with us in all things except sin, was able to make his divine Word into a human word, corresponding to our way of speaking and our forms of expression. The Word of God became incarnate in human language, making itself equal to it in all things except lying. There is no need to have recourse to a direct revelation of God or to an uninterrupted oral transmission to guarantee the truth of this written Word.

The author of the narrative seems to have been a man linked to the current wisdom, i.e., he belonged to the group of people who cared particularly about peoples' lives and the concrete direction of those lives. The horizon of their concerns in the narrative is the family life of the rural dweller. This also is the horizon of a large part of the Wisdom books, at least in their older parts. However, the very marked aspect of denunciation and the wider opening towards the social dimension in chapters 4 to 11 indicate a prophetic interest. The author seems to be at the meeting place of these two currents, both of which existed among the people.

Regarding date of authorship, all agree today that the narrative was written in the tenth century before Christ. Evidence against this is the fact that the great projects of the seventh and eighth centuries seem to be completely unaware of it. Only some much later Wisdom books know and quote it.

The place actually occupied by the narrative in the Bible, i.e., at the beginning of the first book of Moses, does not contradict this theory. Moses lived in the thirteenth century before Christ. But not all the books attributed to St. Augustine were written by St. Augustine. Some are not even from the saint's lifetime. Not all the laws sanctioned by the President and attributed to him are authored by him. The fact that the Paradise narrative was attributed to Moses shows the great authority that it had for the faith of the people.

We cannot discover any more than this about the origin of the narrative. Its author is lost in the shadows of the past. He is anonymous. And indeed it matters little to him and to us. He did not write in order to leave a name. The important thing is to know that God shows himself there and calls upon us. And the narrative, as it in fact exists in the Bible, is clear enough and impressive enough to communicate the divine message—a quite explosive and revolutionary message.

CHAPTER SIX

Meanings for Our Lives

The progress of exegesis and a better knowledge of literary forms show us the way to approach the Paradise narrative and make use of it in our own lives and in catechesis.

The Pontifical Biblical Commission and the Progress of Exegesis

The declarations emanating from the Pontifical Biblical Commission* early in this century on the interpretation of the earthly Paradise and the sin of Adam and Eve should be regarded as strategical commands given on a battlefield, when the battle was at its most critical point. They were very useful, since they led to victory in that battle, even though the war continued and still continues. A strategic command, given in a certain battle, loses its binding power in subsequent battles. It does not have a permanent value, even though it has had an important and valid function.

The Pontifical Biblical Commission itself made other official pronouncements at later dates in which it showed that it was following the new discoveries of science and exegesis, specifically in the field of the interpretation of the first eleven chapters of the Book of Genesis. Listed members of the same commission, in official articles, made it quite clear that the declarations previously made had a provisional and tactical aspect.

---

*This Commission was founded by Pope Leo XIII in 1902, "so that God's words should be given, everywhere among us, that thorough study our times demand and will be shielded not only from every breath of error but even from every rash opinion."

Between February 13, 1905, and June 9, 1953, it issued 23 decrees or *responsa* and two letters (1941 and 1948).

Today, the smoke of those bombs has lifted and the view has become clearer and calmer, at least in those controversial areas. One can see the outline of the horizon, enough to get one's direction. The fight that is being waged today is different. The one who sticks to the terms of the battles of those days, already past, forgets the battle that is going on all around him. He fights for a victory in the past and loses the present battle. He puts final victory in jeopardy. He fights cannons with swords and spears. He applies remedies prescribed during infancy to combat an adult illness. It is no wonder that the sick person dies instead of getting better. It is sad; it is tragic; but it has its funny side.

The decision of Pope Pius XII* which invoked the Catholic doctrine of original sin to forbid the acceptance of polygenism by Catholics is a provisional, not a categorical prohibition. It banned polygenism because, at that time, it was not evident how the dogma of the universality of original sin could be combined with the multiplicity of couples at the origin of the human race. But in this case also the horizon has cleared. It has cleared, not in the sense that now we know how to reconcile the multiplicity of couples with the dogma of the universality of original sin. It has cleared rather in the sense that today we see more clearly that the Bible does not speak of polygenism—neither for it nor against it. It is a problem of the twentieth century that is totally beyond the horizon of the biblical author. The Bible must be explained independently of this problem. Besides, the Pope did not base his affirmation on the direct interpretation of the biblical text but on the traditional view of original sin. This was being questioned and needed a deeper study. The explanation we gave of the sin of Adam and Eve bypasses the problem raised by the Pope and shows that the meaning of original sin neither gains nor loses in value with a possible confirmation of the polygenist theory.

In general, we can say that a dry bandage should not be ripped off a wound. That could make the wound larger than it was before the bandage was applied. At the beginning of the century and in the days of Pius XII it was necessary to protect that weak side of the

---

*In his encyclical *Humani generis*, August 12, 1950.

faith with the bandage of prohibition. Nor could it be permitted that anyone, without qualification, could rip off the bandage by teaching polygenism or other theories, since nothing was clear or defined. The wound would have become larger than before. Since that time many studies have been made which have moistened the bandage. The remedy from the beginning of the century and at the time of Pius XII can be removed without danger. But the wound remains and must be protected with other suitable and efficent remedies.

Paradise: Myth or Reality?

Myth or reality? Fable or history? Unreal or real? These are the questions which remain after all we have said about Paradise. These three questions however, are like three shoots springing from the same trunk, that is, from the same fundamental question: "Was there, or was there not, the sin of Adam?"

The biblical narrative does not pose the problem in these terms. It is not interested in proving whether the *first* man sinned or did not sin. It is interested in calling the reader's attention to the fact that *all* men sin, including the reader, including *us*, including the *first* man, since all of us are Adam, belonging to the same human race and in all of us appears that mysterious and inexplicable tendency towards evil. "If we say we have no sin in us we are deceiving ourselves and refusing to admit the truth" (1 John 1:8).

Because of this the biblical narrative on the sin of Adam is the most real, the most historical, the truest narrative one can find in the Bible, since it tells a story that happens all the time. It tells a story that happens in every age and in all people, those of the present generation just the same as those of the first. And it tells this story not so much to inform as to criticize and awaken, to provoke an effective reaction against evil which springs from that mysterious root anchored in the depths of the human soul and invades the world, filling it with sufferings and ambiguities.

The precise aim of the narrative is to function as a mirror and to confront men with themselves and with their consciences. The one who limits himself to examining the material of the mirror, asking only if it is myth or reality, fable or history, unreal or real, and forgetting to look at himself in this mirror, is twisting the meaning of the narrative. Such a person has thwarted the principal aim of the narrative and will never perceive the errors that God wishes to denounce in one's life by means of the mirror.

From the literary point of view, the narrative may be compared with the mythic and symbolic language of that time. It is a kind of parable, formulated from things that are always happening. It would be more or less like the parables of the Good Samaritan or the Seed, which feature real situations and tell of true and historical things, even though they should not be understood as narratives of the historico-informative type. To attain the end he had in view, the author presented the story of evil in the exact form in which this evil was happening in his time. Because of this he speaks of a Serpent, a tree of life, and a tree of knowledge of good and evil. He speaks of a Garden of Eden and of the other ingredients of the happiness of Paradise, since they were real and true elements of the culture of those times, charged with a real meaning for the people and apt means of communication of the message. Many of these elements do in fact belong to the myths. There is no reason why the Bible should not use mythical elements and speak a mythical language, since mythical language is a human language like all the others, and maybe even richer and fuller of meaning than the others. However, the way in which the Bible speaks of life, of history, of evil, even when it uses mythical language, is completely different from the mentality that inspired and still inspires the other myths. These do not know anything of the faith which admits a personal god; they do not know anything of the hope which tends toward a future guaranteed by God; they do not understand a life dedicated to a cause, the cause of good, to be realized through history.

Thus to limit the discussion of Paradise to a defense against mythical elements would be to invert high order and to fail to see the meaning of the narrative. It would be to fail to understand the deep meaning of the incarnation of the Word of God in human language. This approach would resemble that of the man who enters a movie theater and instead of looking at the picture being projected on the screen watches the hole in the wall through which the beam of light which carries the picture passes. Such a man would never come to understand the message of the film. We are like that. We are so preoccupied with defending the beam of light, i.e., the narrative which carries the message about life, that we do not perceive the call of God which it reveals and projects on the screen of daily life. In the end our defense has neutralized the Bible. We take such good care of the sick man that he ends up dying from too much medical care and we do not even perceive it.

Let us turn now to our original question: myth or reality, fable or history, unreal or real? It is both at once. It is myth and reality. It is fable and history. It is unreal and real. It is true and there is nothing false or erroneous in it. But Paradise as an historical garden never existed. At least, we cannot draw such a conclusion from a biblical basis. Maybe one day science will prove that such a garden did exist. But then the acceptance of the historical existence of this garden at the beginning of the history of the human race will be a result of scientific argument; and it will not be possible to say, "You see, the Bible was right." The Bible has another purpose. The garden of which the Bible speaks would still not be the garden whose existence science had proved. According to the Bible, that which existed still exists, and will exist forever as the real possibility, freely offered by God that man can achieve peace through the support of the power and faithfulness of God. In this sense, the narrative is sheer reality, true history, real and true in the highest degree. And it is on this point that the Bible wishes to be right, and in fact is right.

As we have already said, all the difficulties come from the light we project on the narrative, even before we begin to read it. We think it is a report on the past when, in reality, it is a prophecy of the future, projected into the past.

Paradise Today

As we have seen, the story of Adam and Eve is a real, true story, inasmuch as it describes a happening that is always coming true in every part of the world and in the heart of every man. The way of presenting the story is conditioned by the culture of the time. If the author were living today, his description of Paradise would probably have been different. He would have carefully examined our situation and would have tried to find out where the root and origin of evil is for us today in order to be able to eliminate our ills and open a path to peace.

To get an idea of how his description of Paradise affected his readers, let us imagine a description of Paradise in today's terms which would have the same effect on us that his description had on the readers of that time.

Paradise, or rather the contrasting image of our reality, would be a country, developed in all its sectors. There would be no more need of salaries, since everything would belong to everyone, with everybody sharing actively and responsibly in everything. Everybody would know how to read and write. There would be no illnesses, plagues, or the premature death of children. The working week would be less than forty hours, and all workers would be protected and insured against accidents, which would no longer be possible. The purpose of production would no longer be profit, but rather the individual and collective well-being of all. There would be no exploitation, no foreign domination, no war, no violence. There would be no hold-ups or terrorism, no repression or torture. Individual and collective security would be guaranteed in a way that would eliminate the need for the police and the army. There would be no ghetto slums, no misery, no hunger, no generation gap. Everybody would own his own home, and the towns and cities would have wide roads without dangerous intersections, without accidents, without noise, without pollution. Families would live in peace without infidelity or betrayal, and without domination of the wife and children by the husband. Man would be lord and master of his own evolution. God would be the axis of human life, and his presence would be manifested in all people and in all things. There would be, in short, the most complete harmony, totally different from the situation in which we are actually living.

This description, made in the name of God, would be at the same time a denunciation and an examination of conscience. Readers would perceive through it that the real life situation is not as God wishes it to be. They would feel that to collaborate in maintaining such a situation would be a sin against God, since it would be against the plan he has for men. They would come to a realization of their duty to play their part so that present reality might be transformed into the ideal situation presented in the description of Paradise. They would admit, finally, that such a transformation of present reality would not be possible without the help of God but that, supported by God's will, they could and should work to change the world for the better. Thus, such a description of Paradise would be an effective way of showing people the importance of their faith in God for the life they are living.

In today's terminology Paradise would be like that. It would say to us what the description of Paradise said to the readers of that time. It would have the same impact. And for us the same question would arise: "If the world in which we live is·not as God wants it, then who is responsible for this chaos in which we live? Where is the cause? What are we to do to transform it in accordance with the will of God!" To these questions of ours the Bible does not give answers. What it tries to do is provoke such questions and leave us the job of finding adequate and valid answers, not just theoretical but most of all practical ones, which lead effectively to transformation. Even though the Bible does not give us a concrete recipe for resolving our problem, it does give us a safe orientation in our search for an answer. It lets us know that there is in us a mysterious and inexplicable tendency to evil which is being awakened and activated by our going after the Serpent, and turning away from the living God. It is for us to try to find out who today is fulfilling the role of the Serpent, in order to be able to confront him, crushing his head with our heel.

But maybe today we should begin by leading people to perceive that God is missing from their lives. We have lost the awareness that God should occupy a place in life. The Serpent works today with such efficiency and so subtly that we do not even perceive that we are being sidetracked from the center of our being. As long as we do not perceive this tragic reality of our life, any other remedy for the repair of the world will be a graft onto a dead branch.

Is It Valid Today to Use the Paradise Narrative?

After everything has been said, there arises the question: "Should we then leave aside the narrative of the early Paradise presented by the Bible, and make our own up-to-date description of it?" The answer is not easy.

First of all, to lay aside the Bible narrative as being fictitious, infantile, and out-of-date, or to consider it exclusively as an historico-informative narrative about happenings in the past is, we feel, a sign that we have lost our sensibility for the deeply human and immensely serious value of symbolic and mythical language. It could even be a sign that we are afraid of finding out the true importance of the narrative for our life. Because of this, we try to neutralize it, preferring our own ideas, which are not as dangerous as the message of God.

Besides, it seems neither good nor viable to us to try to rationalize and explain everything. In other words, we do not think it possible to reduce everything to intelligible propositions. This could lead us to forget the great truth that life is a mysterious and irreducible reality which has to do with the mystery of God. We have lost today the ability to speak by means of symbols, and our life is the poorer for it. We have lost the capacity for wonder before life, so necessary for a perception of the mystery of God, which envelops us on all sides, whether it be in the positive aspects or in the negative aspects of life.

I think we should keep these same words of Sacred Scripture and the same symbols. What we should avoid is having such words and symbols explained in a wrong direction, a direction which alienates us from life, by leading us along paths which the Bible does not wish us to follow. Nobody substitutes a commentary for a Shakespearean sonnet, no matter how fine the commentary. It merely serves to create the atmosphere in which the sonnet can function and attain its end. The present commentary has no other aim.

When we expound the faith to others we should not give the hearer or the reader the water already bottled, together with instructions on how to use it. We should rather let him go directly to the spring. Thus he himself can judge if anything has been added to the water, to make it more palatable but perhaps less pure. At times it may be necessary to start by giving bottled water. But the end should always be the same: to attract him in this way to the spring so that he himself may drink there.

It is not the exegete or the catechist alone who has the key to the interpretation of the Bible and the criterion of orthodoxy of faith. Let them give to the people some simple criteria for reading the Bible and trust in the Holy Spirit, who is more intelligent than we and who acts in everyone. Above all let them try to help the people to use the right spectacles in reading Sacred Scripture, since we all have the key to a true interpretation of the gift of life and the gift of the Holy Spirit, who alone succeeds in understanding the things of God and teaches them to men (cf. 1 Cor. 2:9–15).

In all this however, there is demanded, especially today, a wise pedagogy, based not only on distinct ideas, but also and above all on a living faith. As in the Bible, the main concern should always be never to lose the direct and concrete contact with the life that is being lived. When the explanation of the Bible retreats into a theoretical exposition of truths, the life impact of which is not clearly seen, then it is likely that the catechesis is no longer what God is asking of us, however right the ideas may be.

The Bible is a book to be read and to be interpreted. It is not a book to be replaced. No matter how nice our ideas may be, they will never have the guarantee and the force that the words of the Bible have. And this is not merely because it is a divine book, but also because it is a human book, very human, the most human of all books. There is no book that has inspired men more in their progress through life and in their fight for a better world than this book. To miss out on or not to consider this aspect, substituting our own thoughts and ideas for the Bible or parts of the Bible, would be to cut a piece out of our past. And this never happens without loss, since he who cuts a piece out of his past leaves his present opaque and unintelligible. Life is larger than the narrow

limit of our horizon, and longer than the brief span of our existence. Everything in life is relative. The Bible helps us to discover
in life the Absolute of God.

The way in which the student approaches this section of the
Bible is important. It is hard to find the right door by which to enter
the house. He chooses the right way if he comes through a perception of the issues in his own life, and not merely through a reception
of ideas more or less foreign to his mentality. All of this will depend
on the sensitivity of the educator. Therefore, from a pedagogical
point of view, it may be useful and even necessary not to start with
the reading of the Bible, but rather with a reading of the life the
student is living. Only in that way will he perceive that the Bible is
that other wire which, when linked with the wire of life, lights the
lamp and shows the way to travel.

A New Version of the Biblical Text with Commentary

The following is my translation of the biblical text made directly from the Hebrew. We have tried to be faithful, not only to the original text, but also to our own language and culture. Our language has different levels: literary, erudite, common or popular, and vulgar. We have tried to keep to the common, popular level, which is the language used in everyday communication.

The commentary, which runs alongside the translation, indicates merely the general lines of thought and explains the use of one or another word translated in an unusual way. As far as possible, we have tried not to repeat the commentary already given in the preceding pages.

TEXT

2:4–6   4. When God decided to make heaven and earth,
                5. from the earth nothing was growing:
                    neither undergrowth nor cultivated crop.
                    For God had not yet made rain to fall
                    nor yet was there a man
                    to cultivate the fields,

                6. to draw water from the earth
                    and with it irrigate all his tilled land.

COMMENTARY

PARADISE (2:4–6): THE IDEAL CONDITION OF MAN AND THE WORLD AS GOD WILLS IT

Disorder and Chaos (2:4–6): The condition of the world before the creative intervention of God

For people who live in the country, the chaos or disorder that threatens life is drought, lack of irrigation, and the absence of farmers to work the land. This disorder would reduce the land to a desert with no possibility of life. And this is how the author pictures the world before the creative intervention of God: no rain (v. 5), no man to cultivate the earth (v. 5), nobody to carry out irrigation (v. 6).

v. 4   The name *Yahweh* is translated *God.* Yahweh is a proper name that no longer evokes for us what it evoked at that time. A good translation would be *our Lord,* even though this term is today applied almost exclusively to Jesus Christ.

v. 6   Another translation: "There was only the water (vapor, spring?) which *arose* from the earth to irrigate all the surface of the field." The Hebrew permits alternative readings: *arise* or *make to arise* (draw). The second alternative makes better sense. *water, spring,* or *vapor?* The meaning is uncertain. An akkadian word of the same root signifies *water used in irrigation.*

Order Conquers Disorder (2:7–14): God introduces the force of harmony and peace into the chaos

God confronts and conquers the threat of chaos and disorganization: (1) by forming the Man who is to cultivate the fields (v. 7); (2) by planting the orchard which will cover the desert with green (vv. 8–9); and (3) by providing water for irrigation (vv. 10–14). The narrative is not merely describing a unique act already past and gone, but a continuing action which at every instant guarantees life to man.

2:7	7.	Then, God formed the Man, using dust from the field. He breathed in through his nose the breath which gives life, and there was the Man: a living being!
2:8–9	8.	Next, God made an orchard, there in Eden, towards the East, and there he placed the Man whom he had made.
	9.	From the earth he caused every kind of tree to grow, with beautiful and tasty fruits. And, in the middle of the orchard, he caused the tree of life to grow and the tree of knowledge of good and evil.
2:10–14	10.	There in Eden there arises a river, which waters the orchard and then divides into four:
	11.	The first is the Ganges, the one that surrounds all the region of Havilah,
	12.	—the land of gold: very good gold, indeed; the land too of balsam and of precious stones.

FORMATION OF THE MAN (2:7)

v. 7 *Dust, clay:* the Hebrew word indicates the fine dust of the field used by the potters in making delicate objects.
Breath which gives life: Breathing was the sign of life. When it stopped, life ended. The animals too are called *living beings* (Gen. 2:19). The life of man, however, is higher because his breath, i.e., his life, has its origin in a divine breath. He has, by this very fact, the possibility of communicating with God.

PLANTING THE ORCHARD (2:8–9)

v. 8 We translate *orchard,* since it is a garden of fruit trees. *Towards the East:* a geographical indication, purposely left vague. Today we say "up north," "over in Europe." The sense is "an uncertain location," "far from here."

v. 9 *Beautiful and tasty:* Literally, "attractive to look at and good to eat."

THE IRRIGATION WATER (2:10–14)

Verses 10–14 are a parenthesis which give the reader an idea of the fertility and importance of the orchard.

v. 11 The text speaks of *Pishon.* The identification of this river with the Ganges is uncertain. Nor is it possible to identify the region of Havilah.

13. The second river is called the Nile;
    it is the one that flows around Ethiopia.
14. The third river, the Tigris,
    flows over there on the far side of Assyria.
    The fourth is the Euphrates.

2:15   15. So,
    God took the Man
    and placed him in that orchard of Eden,
    so that he might cultivate it
    and take charge of it.

2:16–17   16. And he gave him this order:
    "Of every tree in the orchard
    you may eat, and eat your fill.

v. 13   The text speaks of *Gihon*. The identification of this river
        with the Nile is the most likely meaning.

The Harmony of Life (2:15–24): Man's life and mission in the ideal conditions of Paradise

The narrative now focuses on the man and his life within the
orchard. It describes (1) how he was given responsibility for the
orchard (v. 15); (2) how he received the power of decision over life
and death (vv. 16–17); (3) how he came to have a place of authority
among the other living beings (vv. 18–20); (4) how his matrimonial
and family life was structured (vv. 21–24). Human life ought to be
like this, since this is how God wanted it when he created it.

RESPONSIBILITY FOR THE ORCHARD: TO WORK AND TO CULTIVATE (2:15)

v. 15   Twice, here and in Gen. 2:8, it is said that the man was
        placed in the orchard. God created him outside the or-
        chard. This means that it was not man's nature to live in
        this happiness. It is a free gift offered him by God.

RESPONSIBILITY FOR LIFE: TO FOLLOW THE LAW OF GOD (2:16–17)

v. 16   It is important to note that the divine command covers two
        things: (1) to eat of all the trees, including the tree of life,
        and (2) not to eat of the tree of knowledge of good and evil.
        The command has nothing to do with a period of trial
        during which man's obedience is tested. It deals rather
        with the very condition of human life: to be able to use all
        things, but to use them according to the plan of the
        Creator.

17. Now, from the tree of knowledge of good and evil,
    from that tree do not eat!
    On the day that you eat from it,
    it is certain that you will die!''

2:18–20   18. Then God said:
    ''It is not good that Man remain alone.
    I am going to make for him somebody
    who will help him,
    and who can converse with him.''

19. Then, using earth,
    he formed all the animals and all the birds.
    He brought them to the Man,
    to see how he would call them.
    And the name which the Man gave
    to each living being
    fitted exactly.

20. It was thus
    that the Man gave purpose and name
    to all the animals and birds
    and to all the creatures that live
    in the undergrowth.
    But, for himself, he could not find there
    anyone who would help him and
    who could converse with him.

v. 17   This verse does not imply that there was a poisonous fruit
         which would cause death. As we have seen, this image is
         used to say that the *Order* or *Law of God* places man
         before the choice between life and death (*cf.* Deut.
         30:15–19).

RELATIONSHIP WITH THE ANIMALS:
PLACE OF IMPORTANCE AND DOMINION (2:18–20)

These verses (18–20) are already a preparation for what follows in
vv. 21–24, which speak of the creation and dignity of the woman.
In that culture it was necessary to affirm that woman was equal to
man in dignity. Faith in God led the author to discover so evident a
truth.

v. 18   Literally, "a helper before him," i.e., one who would be
         his equal and not his inferior, who would look him in the
         face and would be able to communicate with him.

v. 19   Literally, "All that man would call the living being, that
         would be its name." To give a name to somebody was the
         equivalent of giving him his purpose, his destiny. It is for
         man to give meaning, purpose, and destiny to all other
         creatures by the use he makes of them. It is as if God
         awaits and depends on man's decision.

v. 20   This describes an ideal situation in which there was no
         enmity between man and the animals. They kept their
         place, serving man and living with him in peace (*cf.* Isa.
         11:6–9).
         It shows too that the animals did not succeed in freeing man
from his solitude, and so prepares for the description of the creation of the woman.

2:21–24   21.   Then God caused the Man
                to fall into a deep sleep.
                While he slept, he drew from him a rib
                and filled in the place with flesh.
          22.   He made the Woman from the rib
                which he had drawn from the Man.

          23.   He brought her to the Man
                and the Man said:
                "Yes, indeed!
                This is bone of my bones,
                and flesh of my flesh."
                For this reason she is called Woman,
                because she was drawn from the Man.

          24.   And so it is that it happens until this day:
                The Man leaves father and mother
                to unite himself with his Woman,
                the two becoming one thing.

2:25   25.   Both the Man and the Woman were naked,
                but they were not ashamed.

MARRIAGE AND FAMILY LIFE: TO MAKE A COMMUNITY (2:21–24)

v. 21 *Deep sleep*: The creative action is God's secret. Only God knows it. Man cannot witness it. This is the meaning of the deep sleep. (*cf*. Ps. 138:13–14; 2 Mac. 7:22).

Rib: As we have already seen, God literally makes real the popular expression "Bone of my bones and flesh of my flesh" (*cf*. v. 23). This is an image to explain that the mysterious attraction of the sexes . . . the unity of matrimony in which the two complete one another come from God. Man should not abuse them.

v. 23 The man recognizes the dignity of the woman, his equal in nature. In Hebrew, this is expressed by a play on words: "For this reason, she is called *issha* (wife), because she was drawn from the *ish* (husband)."

v. 24 *One thing*: Literally, "one flesh alone." This expression does not refer merely to the sexual relationship, but indicates the wider unity which ought to begin and continue to exist between husband and wife in the family. They are to form a real community of life.

Transition to the Second Part (2:25): First reference to the nakedness of the man and the woman

The meaning of this allusion to the nakedness of the man and the woman has already been fully explained. It has nothing to do with sexual abuse. It serves as a biographical indication and prompts the readers to examine their own consciences and discover whether they too might not be Adam or Eve.

1. Now, it so happens that the Serpent is astute,
   the most astute of all the animals
   which God had made.
   And he said to the Woman:
   "So, is it true that God said
   that you may not eat of any tree of the orchard?"

2. The Woman replied:
   "Of course not,
   for we are already eating
   of the fruits of the orchard!

3. It is only of the fruit of that tree
   that God said:
   'Of that one you may not eat
   nor even touch,
   or you will die.' "

4. The Serpent said to the Woman:
   "It is not like that exactly, no!
   You are not going to die, by no means!

SIN (3:1–7): PASSAGE FROM THE IDEAL CONDITIONS OF PARADISE TO THE REAL CONDITIONS OF DAILY LIFE

Temptation (3:1–5): *The Serpent leads men away from following the Law of God*

We have seen that the narrative does not speak of Adam and Eve, but of man and woman. The author of the narrative responds as we do when we want to characterize a whole people. We say, "The German likes to work," "The Brazilian loves football." The narrative tries to characterize the whole human race and refers to "the Man" and "the Woman." What is the attitude of the *man* when he becomes adult and receives the Law of God? The reply is a mirror image of what always happens: (1) He is tempted by the Serpent (vv. 1–5); he accepts the solicitation and falls (v. 6).

v. 1   *The Serpent:* This refers to an enemy already known. We have already explained the meaning of the figure of the Serpent. Here it symbolizes the force of evil, concretized in the magic and superstitious religion of the Canaanites. This religion was the great temptation which led people away from the Law of God.

v. 2   *Of course not:* Literally, "We have eaten of the fruits of the orchard." This categorical affirmation by the woman includes a direct negation of what the Serpent was trying to suggest. The translation makes this negation explicit.

v. 3   The dialogue between the Serpent and the woman shows that both exaggerated the divine command. The Serpent claimed that God had forbidden them to eat of any tree (v. 1). The woman gave the impression that God had prohibited even touching the tree. Neither was being truthful. Starting from false and distorted premises, the conclusion could not be other than false. This lack of truth and objectivity is going to trigger the temptation.

5.   It is just that God knows that
     the day on which you eat from that tree
     you are going to open your eyes
     and are going to be equal to him:
     You will have knowledge of good and evil.''

3:6   6.   The Woman, then, looked at the tree:
              How delightful!
              How marvellous!
              How she wanted to achieve this knowledge!
              She seized the fruit and ate,
              gave it to her husband who was with her,
              and he too ate.

3:7   7.   Then, the eyes of both were opened
              and they saw that they were naked.
              They put together fig leaves
              and made loincloths.

v. 5   *To be as gods:* The eternal temptation of man is to refuse
to recognize himself as a creature before the Creator. He
revolts against his condition of radical dependence and
tries to surpass his limitations by making himself a god and
by considering himself the unique, exclusive, and absolute
norm of good and evil. The root of sin lies in the erroneous
option that man takes before God. Man refuses to place
himself in his rightful position before the Creator. He
refuses to be clay in the hands of the potter.

The Fall of the Woman and the Man (3:6): *They fall because they want to be more than they can be*

v. 6   Literally, "And the woman saw that the tree was good to
eat, desirable to the eyes, covetable on account of the
knowledge." The Serpent did not take away the woman's
responsibility. He merely aroused her desire and curios-
ity. Then he disappeared.

The woman presents the fruit to her husband, who also
eats. The two share in the evil, as indeed all men share in
the evil that touches them. It is no use trying to cast the
blame onto others. Each will pay for the evil he has done
(*cf.* Exod. 18:1–32).

Transition to the Third Part (3:7): *Second reference to the nakedness of the man and the woman*

For the significance of nakedness, see the commentary above
(2:25).

3:8–10   8.   They heard the footsteps of God
            as he took a walk in the orchard,
            at the time of the evening breeze.
            But the Man and the Woman
            did not show themselves.
            They remained hidden among the trees
            of the orchard.
       9.   Then, God called out to the Man:
            "Where are you?"
      10.   He replied:
            "I heard your footsteps in the garden,
            but I was afraid, because I am naked.
            And I went to hide."

3:11–13   11.   God said:
            "How did you find out that you were naked?
            You must have eaten of that tree,
            in spite of my prohibition.
            Didn't you?"

      12.   The Man replied:
            "It was the Woman whom you gave me
            as a companion;
            it was she who gave me the fruit of that tree,
            and I ate."

PUNISHMENT (3:8–24): THE REAL, EVERYDAY CONDITIONS OF HUMAN EXISTENCE

Change of Relationship with God (3:8–13): Fear and desire to flee felt by the guilty before the Judge

The first reaction of the man, after he has sinned, is the realization of being guilty before God. This realization is expressed (1) in his fear and desire to flee when God appears (vv. 8–10), and (2) by recognition of God as his Judge, with authority to set up an inquiry that will establish responsibility (vv. 11–13).

FEAR AND FLIGHT BEFORE GOD (3:8–10)

v. 8   Another possible translation: "They heard the voice of God that resounded in the orchard at the end of the day." In both cases, there is a perception of the presence of God, felt no longer as a reason for joy and closeness, but as a reason for fear as one awakens to his fault. At the moment God appears, man perceives that he is not as he should be (*cf.* Gen. 32:31; Exod. 19:21; 33:20; Deut. 5:24).

v. 10   It is not God who cut off the relationship. It is man who perceived, within himself, that something has changed radically in his relationship with God. He feels the presence of God as a judgment (*cf.* Job 3:19–21).

GOD, AS JUDGE, INVESTIGATES THE RESPONSIBILITY (3:11–13)

v. 11   In the perception of nakedness a new awareness of man before God is revealed. Cut off from God, man no longer encounters himself, becoming a stranger to himself. His shame at his nakedness expresses this

v. 12   Confronted by God, man recognizes his fault, but tries to diminish his responsibility, alleging that he was led into the act by the woman. Indirectly, he blames God for giving him the woman as companion.

13. Then God said to the Woman:
     "How could you have done such a thing?"
     The Woman replied:
     "The Serpent deceived me,
     and I ate."

3:14–15   14. Then God said to the Serpent:
                "Because you have done this,
                you will be accursed,
                separated from all the animals.
                You will have to crawl on your belly,
                you will have to eat the dust of the earth,
                forever!
           15. I am going to bring about enmity
                between you and the Woman,
                between your race and hers.
                She will crush your head
                and you will be able to attack her
                only by the heel."

v. 13   The inquiry draws to a close, getting to the root of the evil
          that has been done. The Serpent, that is, the temptation of
          magic, awoke in man that inexplicable urge to be like God
          and to deny his own rightful condition as a human crea-
          ture.

The Punishment Brought on by the Fault (3:14–19): *The ambiguity of everyday reality becomes a call from God*

Once responsibility has been assigned, it is the time for sanctions:
(1) against the Serpent (vv. 14–15), (2) against the woman (v. 16),
and (3) against the man (vv. 17–19). The situation created by the
divine sentence is the real situation in which the reader recognizes
his daily life experience which is in opposition, point by point, to
the ideal situation of Paradise. In this way, the author interprets
the ambiguous reality of life, linking this reality with a call from
God for conversion.

SENTENCE ON THE SERPENT (3:14–15)

vv. 14, 15   The meaning of these two verses has already been
               sufficiently explained in the commentary (pp. 46–47).

3:16   16.   And he said to the Woman:
               "Now must I indeed multiply
               your sufferings:
               You will have to become pregnant often,
               and it is with pains that you will bring forth
               your children.
               You will be drawn to your husband,
               and he will dominate you!"

3:17–19   17.   And to the Man he said:
                "You listened to your wife
                and ate of the tree,
                in spite of my prohibition.
                Because of this
                the earth will be accursed on account of you.
                Only with great difficulty
                will you succeed in drawing from it
                your sustenance,
                all your life long.

          18.   Thorns and briars will it produce.
                You will have to eat of the herbs of the fields.

          19.   You will have to sweat
                to be able to eat your bread.
                And all this
                until you return to the earth,
                for from it you were drawn.
                Dust you are!
                Dust you are going to remain!"

SENTENCE ON THE WOMAN (3:16)

v. 16   Literally, "I will multiply, indeed, your conceptions."
For the meaning of the frequent pregnancies and the begetting of children, see the commentary (p. 46).

This verse enumerates the evils connected with human
love, maternity, and family life. The Bible interprets them
as a situation of divine punishment, i.e., as an abnormal
situation. Life should not be like that. Accordingly, these
evils forbid a fatalistic passivity and remind us of the need
for conversion.

SENTENCE ON THE MAN (3:17–19)

v. 17   The description of the punishment, in these verses, is
provocative and revolting. This is so that man, awakening
to his responsibility, may no longer consider his actual
situation as normal and definitive.

Enumerated here are the evils of work and of the
human condition in general: drought, working for subsis-
tence which is difficult and bears little fruit, the ungrateful,
unproductive earth, sickness and death, scarce and insufficient food. Everything is interpreted as a situation of
punishment, with which man cannot compromise but
which is going to last as long as man has not paid his debt to
God.

v. 18   Previously, man ate only the "beautiful and tasty" fruits
of the orchard. Now he must eat the "herbs of the field,"
an inferior form of sustenance, linked with the tiring job of
cultivating the land.

v. 19   With this insistent allusion to inevitable death, the sentence ends. Death is the great mystery that calls into
question the meaning of life. Any realistic interpretation
of life must start with the inevitable fact of certain and
universal death. It is from this point that the author now
proceeds.

3:20   20.   The Man called his wife Eve,
                      since she is the mother of all men.

3:21   21.   God made clothes of skin
                      for the Man and the Woman
                      and with them he clothed them.

Conclusion (3:20–24): *Life begins again, realistically and hopefully*

Most characteristic of man is his desire to live forever, in spite of the inevitability of his dying some day: 1. In this condition, his only way of getting past this barrier of death is by procreation (v. 20). 2. In this life, he can and must count on the help of God (v. 21). 3. But he has no way of avoiding death at his disposal (v. 22). 4. He must face up to the hard reality of life, accept his condition, and resist it, in the hope that one day he may have life as a gift of God (vv. 23–24).

THE BEGINNING OF THE HISTORY OF MANKIND IN SEARCH OF LIFE (3:20)

v. 20   For the first time the name *Eve* appears, a symbolic name indicating the role of the woman: to be a mother. For the first time procreation is spoken of—after death has entered in. Procreation is seen as a way to overcome death and prolong one's life through children.

MAN CAN COUNT ON GOD (3:21)

v. 21   God did not break with man. He keeps on protecting him, helping him to cover his nakedness, i.e., by his love God awakens man to his own worth, making him come out of his nakedness and nothingness.

3:22   22. And God said:
               "Let's see now!
               The Man has now become like us;
               he knows good and evil!
               He must not be allowed, then,
               to stretch out his hand
               to pick also from the tree of life,
               to eat of its fruit
               and live forever!''

3:23–24   23. Therefore he ordered him out
               of the orchard of Eden
               to work the earth,
               from which he had been drawn.

          24. God expelled the Man and made him live
               on the eastern side of the orchard of Eden.
               He placed the cherubim and the sword
               to guard the way
               that leads to the tree of life.

DEATH IS INEVITABLE (3:22)

v. 22   This is said with irony. The man got what he wanted. To the wisdom of the Law of God he preferred his own wisdom, and instead of life he found death. Such a situation cannot be reversed. Life, however, is still a possibility since the tree of life was not destroyed. But God has blocked access to it. In the present situation, there is no magic by which man could lay hold on life. The only way leading to life is through death. In this narrative there appears the first ray of faith in the resurrection and hope for a life with God which would conquer death.

REALITY: THE CERTAINTY OF DEATH AND THE HOPE OF LIFE (3:23–24)

v. 23   The reality of man is this: For him, now, Paradise does not exist. There exists a hard life with daily trials constantly reminding him of death (*cf.* Gen. 3:19).

v. 24   *Cherubim:* An image drawn from Babylonian mythology, in which there is mention of *karibu,* a hybrid animal composed of elements of man, lion, eagle, and bull. It represents a very strong being, one that cannot be overcome by man. It indicates man's inability to continue to live by his own powers. This being blocks the approach of man to the tree of life. *Sword:* Literally, "flame of the flashing blade." Just as the rainbow was interpreted as a sign of God's friendship with man (*cf.* Gen. 9:8–17), so the lightning that appears in storms should remind man of his condition as a mortal creature. It is, as it were, the sword of God.

Therefore man should abandon superstition and the practice of the fertility cult, which express an unworthy effort to attain immortality; he should rather follow the Law of God. From this will spring the hope of life, which pervades the entire Bible, and which blossoms fully in the resurrection of Christ. The resurrection, going beyond death, is Paradise finally realized.

CHAPTER SEVEN

Speaking of Original Sin

In this final chapter we try to bring together the loose and scattered pieces of the preceding pages to present a more coherent picture of what has been said about original sin. Perhaps we will repeat some things already said but it will be a useful repetition since it will help us to see that the doctrine of original sin is much richer and reveals many more things about life than we might suspect.

We will begin with a short description of the usual, popular view we have today of original sin. It is a view that gives rise to many questions: it has little to do with life and gets little support from the Bible.

We will try to present, in five points, the thought of the biblical author concerning the origin of the evil we call original sin. We will point out the way in which our reflection on this problem has been sidetracked. It is here that we will have to repeat some things previously stated.

Finally, we will try to clarify, in three points, the questions that arise from our explanation of the Paradise narrative; these are questions for which the narrative has no answer since they are beyond the horizon of its author.

Our Customary, Popular View of Original Sin

The biblical author did not write his narrative to prove our doctrine of original sin. When he wrote, he knew nothing about what we would one day deduce from his words. On the other hand, our doctrine of original sin does not have its only basis in the biblical narrative about the sin of Adam. It does not even have its firmest foundation there. If we did not have the letters of the

Apostle Paul along with the interpretation of them made by the Fathers of the Church and if we did not have the polemics with the Pelagians and the Protestants which provoked the official pronouncements of the Councils, the knowledge of original sin that we have today would never have matured in the Church.

However, in the course of the long reflection of Christians on the origin of evil, some aspects have been stressed while others have been allowed to slip into oblivion. For example, in order to explain the dogma of the universality of original sin, Christians had recourse to the concept of its hereditary transmission. But by doing this original sin was separated, at least in people's minds, from the personal sin that each person commits. We forgot to consider the very close connection that exists between original and personal sin. Original sin, for many, has become a kind of sticker that one puts on defective goods when they leave the factory: "Beware! Not for export!" It has been reduced to a production defect that passes from father to son, without any possibility of interference. Detached in this way from the life of responsibility which the person leads, original sin has become a loose piece in life, one that we do not know what to do with. And, without realizing it, we shake our head in God's direction and say, "He might have made a better product."

Because of this, today original sin raises a whole series of questions about things which are completely beyond the reach of our powers of observation and verification, and which mean so little to the life we live. How can a child have a sin, if he never sinned? What can baptism take away from a child who is not able to take anything on. How could God have made the misery of all of us depend on the sin of one couple? Was he not unjust? Why do we have to suffer today the consequences of a fault we did not commit, against which we could not defend ourselves, and of which we have no awareness or memory? Where does the child go who dies before baptism? He cannot go to heaven, since he is in sin. He cannot go to hell, since he did not sin. The conclusion was reached that there must exist some kind of intermediate place, which we called limbo. But for this conclusion of ours there is no argument in the Bible. However, it is a logical conclusion, drawn from the premises we posited about original sin. This leads us to question the correctness of the premises. When the final conclusion is wrong, the error should be sought in the premises. Do we really interpret aright the dogma of original sin and its universality?

On this account it is useful to pose very clearly the terms within which the author expounds the problem. Instead of looking in the Bible for a confirmation of our ideas, let us rather look for a safe criterion for criticizing with objectivity these ideas of ours, not all of which are dogmas of faith.

The Thinking of the Biblical Author on the Origin of Evil

He sets out to look for the source that is causing evil in the world today. As we have already said, the biblical author does not prove the existence of original sin in the same terms in which we today understand this sin. He has a different point of view. He noted the evils of family and social life around him. He was against them. His deepest faith was that God could not be the author of this widespread malaise. Thus, starting with the oil slick on the surface, he went on to seek its origin. He looked not so much into the past, but rather into the inner depths of man. And there in fact he found the root, the capital vice of humanity, which explained to him this widespread disorder. He noted in all people a mysterious and inexplicable tendency to break with God. It manifested itself at the moment they arrived at adulthood, when they had to assume responsibility before God, before themselves, and before others for their lives and acts. At this moment, men broke with God by not choosing to live life as they should and proclaimed their would-be independence before the Creator. They did not want to be "vessels of clay in the hands of the potter." They left the Law of God to follow their own law. The tree revolted against the fact of its being made of wood.

The author's judgment on the origin of evil, formulated in the cultural terms of his time, touches all men. The author was thinking in terms of the human race, since he spoke of Adam, Man.

The author did not exclude anyone from his judgment, neither ourselves nor the first man. However, his analysis of the human race was made through the spectacles that were his as a Hebrew, living at that time. And in that concrete situation, the Hebrews' break with God was manifested in their following the Serpent.

Thus the author does not break the bond linking personal sin with what we call original sin. It is in our personal sin that the origin of evil appears and awakens in us. Personal sin reveals, activates, confirms, and increases that root of evil. Unfortunately, in our past thinking on original sin, we lost our sensitivity for its real, personal aspect. We posed the problem almost exlusively in terms of time and history, limiting ourselves to asking, "How did this vice enter into the human race? What has come down to us as a result and consequence of the sin of our first parents?" The biblical author does not think in such terms. He does not relate how the vice entered, but how it was in fact entering and proliferating. He indicates the point of short circuit between God and man that was throwing the world into inescapable darkness. For the author, the first man and we today are in identical circumstances. There exists in all of us a mysterious and inexplicable abyss of evil. From this abyss, the evil breaks out on the surface and shows itself in our personal sins. At the very root of our being we are cut off from God; all of humanity is at fault, although individuals may not be aware of this. Deep within us, the plug is disconnected from the circuit that originates in God. When we reach the stage of being able to flick the switch, the bulb does not light up. Then, instead of plugging in the lamp, we keep on flicking the switch, demonstrating and approving of the darkness in which we find ourselves and for which we are responsible.

The author seeks the origin of evil in order to eliminate it. The author sets out to seek the origin of evil, not just to possess this knowledge, but to be able to react, to be able to apply a remedy and so to resist efficiently. If the lamp of life does not light, then somewhere we should be able to find the cause. He seeks the cause, not simply to know that the cord is not plugged into the socket deep inside man, thus enabling him to return home satisfied with having found out the cause. If he seeks the cause, it is because he wants to put the plug back in the socket. He wants to return home satisfied that the light has returned which allows him to see the face of the other.

We have lost our sensitivity with regard to this. We are satisfied with knowing how the evil entered into life. Our theological reflection does not have the eminently practical aspect which characterizes the Bible narrative. We are like a group of people forming a circle around the victim of a road accident. They hold a lively discussion about how it happened and who was or was not to blame. In the meantime, the victim is bleeding and dying before their eyes without assistance. We were of the opinion that knowledge alone would resolve the problem. And we even fought and killed because of it. But this Socratic style of philosophy does not solve the problems.

The author of the biblical narrative thinks in other terms. If it was possible for free acts of men to bring forth this spring of evil, then it should still be possible for the free acts of men to seal off this spring of evil. It was the hope of conquering evil that led man to reflect on the presence of evil.

What Was the Basis of the Author's Hope?

To repair man and the world is possible only through the power of God, since only the power of God is stronger than the power of evil. The biblical author does not believe that man can realize his duty of eliminating evil with his own natural capacity. Man does not have the strength needed for this. Left to himself, he is not able to repair life and the world. Besides, talking about the natural capacity of man did not even occur to the author. It occurred to men and to Christians only when the Pelagians, following the legalistic line of the Pharisees, brought up this possibility.

For the biblical author it is a clear and almost self-evident truth that Paradise can be built only with the help of the power of God. And this is not because Paradise is beyond the horizon of man's natural power, but because evil is in a certain sense anterior to man and radically dominates him. Evil is stronger than man. Man is born already wrapped up in it. Daily experience witnesses to this even today. It would seem that man is born crooked, even though this shows itself only when he reaches the age of responsible choice. Only then what lies dormant in man makes its appearance. Only then does it become evident that the lamp is unplugged. Only then does the cancerous virus awaken to begin its destruction by means of the free decision of the man who sins. Vice begins to be vice indeed, and becomes personal. Man thus confirms which side he wants to be on. And all men choose the same side, since all sin. Man, by himself, does not have the strength to seal off the spring of evil that gushes up within him.

But though evil may be strong, even stronger than man, it does not conquer man. This is the author's belief and it is from this faith that his hope and his will to fight springs. God is there to help man in his choice of the good side and to keep that vice from taking charge of his heart. God is there to tear out the evil, root and all, in a way that will definitively keep man from doing evil. God showed this power and conquered evil in the resurrection of Christ. This, of course, the author did not know. But he already had an intuition of it: there could be no evil in the earthly Paradise which he described in his prophecy of the future, and the progeny of the Woman would win a future victory over the Serpent which would be crushed. The author is an optimist and full of hope, since, in the context of the plan of God, he thinks that evil will not succeed in causing much damage. It will be no more than a "scratch in the heel" (Gen. 3:15).

This strength of God is not something that is added on to man. It is born within him and lifts up his strength to a higher potential. The strength of the resurrection is not a foreign body, a type of reserve engine, but is man's very own strength, lifted up to its highest potential, which only God knows and can activate by the love that he communicates (*cf.* Eph. 1:17–21).

The hour of temptation. This mysterious potentiality for evil which is inherent in the very liberty of man appears and goes into action at the hour of temptation. At this time it seems as if the whole world concentrates its forces, in the image of the Serpent, to lead man to evil, cutting him off from God. As long as a man has not yet reached manhood, he has not yet defined his position. He has not yet chosen which side he is going to be on. However, the choices made by others before him create an environment from which the isolated individual escapes with difficulty. He will be conquered by the temptation which falls upon him from outside and from inside. The evil which is mysteriously born from within man and which springs up from his consciousness, also bursts forth from his life structures and social life. Thus is there in man himself and in the world which surrounds him a protest against God and against what is good. The way of evil has become, for humanity, the natural way, so natural that the malignant tumor which attacks the organism hides under the skin and does not appear. Men are not aware of the evil nor of the temptation to which they are subject—a tragic situation which has no remedy unless man awakes, becomes aware of his situation before God, and starts to react, supported by the power of God.

This is the end that the author wishes to reach with his narrative. He wants to give his readers greater awareness of the temptation to which they are subject and to which they are yielding, by their unwitting exchange of Paradise for a troubled life of suffering.

This is the interpretation of the evil that exists in the world given us by the author of the biblical narrative. There arise for us now, out of this interpretation, various questions which were at that time beyond the horizon of the author. There is nothing to keep us from asking such questions and trying to find an answer that will satisfy us, without having to distort what the Bible affirmed and what the faith of the Church today puts before us as true.

Reply to Our Questions

Moving on from the interpretation given up to now, we ask the following questions: So man was created twisted? Otherwise how could there arise in him that mysterious tendency towards evil? What, in fact, is this tendency to evil? If the biblical author is thinking in terms of adult man, what fault does the newborn child have? Why baptize children? Would it not be better, then, to baptize them when they reach the adult age of which the author speaks?

We are not going to respond to the concrete terms of the questions, but we will present three fundamental considerations that will offer sufficient elements to supply a response, or at least the way to a response.

We are born with a radical maladjustment in relation to the end for which we were created. Trying to reply within the mentality of the biblical narrative, we think that we can say the following: Man was created by God for a destiny that is beyond the horizons which man himself could see during his human existence. He was placed within the garden. He was not born in it. All that there is within man tends to go beyond the limited horizons which cut off our view. This is the condition in which man lives. The biblical author does not know any other condition nor any other destiny. He—and indeed this is true for all the Bible—never reflected in terms of a natural destiny, of life in the state of "pure nature." He does not make a distinction between natural destiny and supernatural destiny, as if they were two distinct things, one stuck on top of the other without internal unity. Our destiny is one and only one Paradise: life with God. This destiny is inscribed in the very being of man and reveals itself in a thousand ways in daily life. Everything in man says, "I was made for higher things." Man is not trash that comes defective from the factory. He is up to export standard and was destined for it. He was destined to surpass himself. He was made for God. "And our heart will be restless until it rests in God" (Saint Augustine).

Because of this, it is not enough for man to be born of man, he must be born also of God (*cf.* John 1:13; 3:5). And it is at this point that man, arriving at the age of awareness, fails. The failure at adulthood reveals something about the very destiny of man. It shows that our heart is bigger than ourselves. We do not succeed in filling it. It reveals that radical maladjustment with which we were born. That is, to the extent to which man's consciousness opens up, it opens up towards the infinite; and to this same extent man

discovers, necessarily, the limits of his possibility of attaining this
infinite. It is not an error of production. Man does not carry within
himself any awareness of some fault previously committed. He
does not carry with him the sin of his parents as if it were his own
personal sin. Personal evil starts when man, instead of opening
himself to this infinite and, being born of God,who stretches out his
hand to him, tries to reduce the infinite to the size of his own finite
limits. And so he creates the illusion that he himself is his own god.
Personal evil begins when man tries to be "equal to God" (Gen.
3:5). With this attitude, man introduces into life and into the world
the germ of disorder and disintegration which vitiates things at
their root. Thus, everything that is born of the man who acts in this
way is turned away from God at its very root. This attitude,
practiced and maintained throughout the whole historical evolution of the human race, has created a whole structure that is out of
joint. The evil no longer appears only from within, but lies in wait
for man on every side. It becomes so natural that we no longer
perceive the root of this disorder that surrounds and afflicts us.

*There exists among men a mysterious solidarity in evil; and in
all of us there is an absolute need of redemption and
liberation.*   Why does man reveal this failing when he reaches
manhood? What is this mysterious tendency to evil? Man is involved in guilt before he comes to the use of the reason. Here we
must admit our ignorance before the mystery of evil and life. Our
anxiety to explain everything brings with it the real danger of
rationalization, which succeeds in eliminating and obscuring even
the most evident things. There is in us a mystery which cannot be
explained but which is imposed on everyone's consciousness with
an almost brutal violence.

We seek out thousands of explanations for it, but in reality such
explanations are not more than castles in the air which do not stand
up to realistic trial. These ideas and explanations of ours burst like
the most beautifully colored soap bubbles when they touch the
earth of the reality of life. We are dealing with the mysterious
solidarity of all of us in evil. How many limitations have we not
suffered because others sinned and are still sinning? How

much do others suffer because of our culpable and nonculpable limitations? And which nonculpable limitation does not have a culpable origin in the past, be it of ourselves or others? We are dealing, too, with the need we all *feel* for redemption, whether we have a clear awareness of this need or a conscious desire for redemption or not. Our heart has aspirations which surpass us and which we cannot realize. And it is the faith of the Church that this "we cannot" exists, not because Paradise is beyond our horizon, but that it is rather a result of a fault of man. That radical maladjustment of ours regarding the end that attracts us does not exist in us without our being to blame.

There is a sin, there is a fault stamped on the face of humanity which cries so much and so loudly that we have become used to its cry. We are like workers who have become used to the noise of their machines. We do not even hear the cry that accuses us. And for this guilt *all of us* are jointly liable, boys and girls, old people and children. We are jointly liable, simply by belonging to the same human race. Nobody can divest himself of his body and make himself comfortable in the face of evil. Nobody can rise up as a pure accusor of the evils that exist in others. We must all sit in the chair of the accused. This joint liability for evil touches all men in time and in space.

There was a time when this awareness of joint responsibility for evil was so strong that men used to find it normal to kill the son for the sin of the father. But through the prophet Ezekiel, God helped them to put things in their proper perspective. Personal punishment is to be for personal guilt (Ezek. 18:1–32). But everyone bears the punishment for the guilt which is everyone's, and to which everyone contributes by his personal sins.

Such language is hard, aggressive, and provocative; but this is the interpretation which we give of evil, in the light of our faith. The Christian does not seek to impose his vision as if it were the only sure one. He offers it as his contribution to help towards the correct analysis of reality. It is the tranformation of reality, made in accordance with the previous analysis, that helps to show the value and the exactness of the vision which the Christian offers to the world. Because of this, the Christian cannot confine himself to mere analysis, to a theoretical statement of facts. He must set about a realistic transformation of the world and of life.

But how can anyone, in good conscience, attribute guilt to a newborn child? One does not attribute any personal guilt to the child such as would merit personal punishment. But the child has entered into a world where neutrality no longer exists. What is born of man alone is already turned away from God at its root. Our greatest evil is to live in neutrality, thinking that good and evil are merely the two verges of a wide road that goes forward in neutrality. We no longer are aware of our real joint liability for the evil and the guilt which today exist, organized and structured, involving everything and everybody, like the air we breathe. And we breathe the air without realizing it. The power of evil which oppresses, makes infantile, massifies, and crushes is so strong that there is no human power capable of facing up to it, unless it be the strength which is born in man emanating from God.

The meaning of baptism: the new solidarity in goodness.   The question as to whether it is right to baptize children arises when one divides the world into three parts: good, bad, and indifferent. But in reality there are only two parts: good and bad. Everything we do contributes, whether we like it or not, to goodness or evil, to the life or the death of humanity. Indifference is not possible. The apparent indifference in which so many try to live is the greatest evil we could imagine. Indifference is itself a stand.

In the face of everyone's solidarity in evil and guilt, which draws humanity ever farther from Paradise, God places a solidarity in good, stronger than evil. The launching pad of this solidarity in good should be the group of people associated with Christ by baptism. In the death of Christ it became apparent how tremendous and how self-destructive is the force of evil. But in his resurrection it was proved that with the force of God it is possible to eliminate evil and build Paradise. And so baptism links man with Christ and enables him to oppose evil successfully. Baptism is his commitment to the group which believes in the plan of God and which tries to realize it through history, expecting from God as much help as is required, through Jesus Christ.

Baptism, we say, removes original sin. And we speak correctly, though we interpret badly. It removes original sin inasmuch as it gives man the ability to fight victoriously against the evil within himself and in the world, until he has eliminated the root from which it all comes. Baptism is not just a washing which another person does for us while we passively stand by. It is a washing which Christ begins in us and which we continue in ourselves and in the world, supported by his strength, which is born in us in this way. The final result of this washing or transformation is Paradise.

What is this strength which springs up in us and by which we can victoriously confront evil? The secret of the superiority of our solidarity in good over our solidarity in evil lies in the creative strength of love which God succeeds in releasing in the hearts of men through his pardoning of our sins. "This is the love I mean: not our love for God, but God's love for us when he sent his son to be the sacrifice that takes our sins away" (1 John 4:10). Jeremiah, too, bases the new relationship with God on pardon: "There will be no further need for neighbor to try to teach neighbor or brother to turn to brother, saying: 'Learn to know Yahweh!' No, they will all know me, the least no less than the greatest . . . since I will forgive their iniquity and never call their sin to mind" (Jer. 31:34). This love which manifests itself in pardon brings man back to himself. Man finds himself, awakens to his own world, and is born again, overcoming the force of evil which kept him confined within himself as a prisoner of his egoism. This new awareness he receives from God, and is made explicit in baptism.

If that is so, then why baptize a child who is in no way aware of all this? Here it is fitting to make two observations:

First, the adult also would not have any awareness of these things, if it did not spring up in him as a free gift of God. The initiative for true liberation comes from the greater love of God, which awakens us to our true worth. In this light, the adult is on the same footing as the child. Neither one can merit what God is working in him. But somebody might reply, "If I cannot merit this gift, at least I ought to be able to assume it by a radical revolution of life. And the child is not able to make such an option."

Secondly, when *does* man make a mature and radical option? Could it be that the same thing happens with the human option as happens with the fragile threads which together make a strong rope, strong enough to pull a truck? Or as happens with the thousands of bricks which together make a house? Does the last brick build the house? Does the last thread make the rope strong? No! The mature human option seems to be the very intricate and complex bundle of little decisions that we go on making throughout life, from childhood on. And when can one say that a man has placed the last brick in the construction of his house? When is he ripe for the definitive option demanded by baptism? Life seems to be a tortuous journey of constant choosing. Continually we are at the fork in the road, between good and evil, in this progressive journey from unconscious childhood to conscious adulthood.

The real root of the problem about the baptism of children is not so much in the children as in we who are adults. It is we who do not know exactly what to do with our baptism. It is we who live too much in indifference, in this neutral median strip between the two lanes, where no car runs. In realilty, this median does not even exist along the road of life. It is we who do not have enough awareness of our joint liability for evil and of our absolute need for redemption. We are not aware of the forces that are engaged in the fight between good and evil, nor do we feel really involved in this battle. We are not aware that we belong to the group which ought to be the launching pad for humanity in the building of Paradise. And if this is the real root of the problem, then our discussion as to whether it makes sense to baptize children will never end, nor will it have meaning except for ourselves. And indeed,it does not seem very recommendable to confer baptism on a child whose parents are not concerned about these problems, not because of the child, since he is incapable of making a choice, but because of the parents who have not made a choice. And from this point of view, it is good that the baptism of children be discussed, since the discussion which goes on while the child is asleep helps to awaken the parents.

The above are some considerations about original sin. They are incomplete. They merely seek to help bring into our lives a little more of the truth we carry within us and do not know quite what to do with. This is so much the case that the high point of the discussion about original sin seems to be the fate of children who die without baptism. Let us leave to the mercy of God the fate of these children, since the mercy of God is, without doubt, greater and stronger than all our ideas about them.

As we already suggested, the problem of the baptism of children and original sin is a partial problem, in which there is revealed the *great problem* which affects us today. We just do not know what to do with our faith in this new world which is emerging. The Church, this little flock, does not exist for itself, but for others. As long as it has not taken a realistic stand in the face of *the others,* it will be without an identity, not knowing who it is or why it exists or what it is supposed to do; and it will not discover the meaning of the truths it carries in the portfolio of faith.

The partial problem of the baptism of children and original sin will be more clearly resolved the day we confront the world of today with the same realism that characterizes the biblical description of Paradise. At that moment we will rediscover, in a new and vital way, the meaning of the ancient truth about sin and baptism.

A Summary, a Norm, a Secret

The Summary

The description of the earthly Paradise and original sin is a public confession of the real responsibility and blame with regard to the evils existing in the world. It is an appeal for a transformation of the world for the better, beginning with life itself by linking it anew with God. It is a declaration of nonconformity, a cry of hope. In the very hour at which the death of man is decreed, there arises for him the hope of life forever. It is only when death ceases to be a natural part of existence and becomes a real problem that the meaning of life will begin to be questioned. Only then will man seek a support for his hope and, according to the Bible, he can find it in God.

The Norm

At the end of all these explanations, some readers may be happy and satisfied with what has been said. In fact, we have corrected some points of view, eliminated some futile difficulties, and tried to reply to the questions raised by common sense and science. All this was done with the sole intention of helping the Word of God to *function* with its light and strength. However, the correctness of these explanations will be proved only by the way in which the Word of God begins to function in our lives. If our explanation leads us to ask new questions, this time questions much more serious and all-embracing, much more troublesome and involving than the questions we listed at the beginning of this book, if we start to be a little more dissatisfied with ourselves and with the general situation in which we live; if already we do not accept everything so naturally; if we have become a little more critical and more humble in the face of reality; if we have been thrown back on ourselves and on our life; if we have begun to be a bit more worried about the evil that exists around us; if we have begun to absolutize a little less our own ideas and to believe a little more in the strength of God or if, at least, we have begun to suspect that he represents some value previously unknown to us—then the Word of God has begun to act and we are within sight of the end he wishes to achieve in us by this biblical narrative. This is the norm.

The Secret

This explanation of the earthly Paradise and Adam's sin is not new; it is not "progessive" or modern. We have not related anything new. All that we have said is old; it was already in the Bible, waiting for somebody to discover it. And it has always been discovered, by each epoch in its own way. We merely tried to change the spectacles with which we were accustomed to read and interpret the narrative. For the one who has changed his spectacles, the old becomes new. The narrative that appeared to be alien, raising questions that alienated still more, has now come within the immediate horizon of our life. Maybe it has entered to such an extent that one or another might prefer not to have learned of it. The *secret* of the explanation and understanding of the Word of God, at least as far as concerns the concrete situation in which we live today, seems to us to consist, not in great erudition or in scientific information about the things of the past, but in the deepening of the life we are living today and through which we are linked with the past and the future. This life is the doorway by which we ought to begin to act in concert with God. If not, then our explanation is an attempt to put oil paint on a damp wall. It doesn't stick; it forms blobs and falls off. It is old even before it is new. But all that enters through the doorway of life, life lived intensely, is new and of immediate interest, no matter how old and antiquated it may appear.

Bibliography

Bonhoeffer, Dietrich. *Creation and Fall: A Theological Interpretation of Genesis 1–3.* Trans. John C. Fletcher. New York: Macmillan, 1959.

Bright, John. *A History of Israel.* London: SCM, 1960.

Cassuto, Umberto. *A Commentary on the Book of Genesis.* Trans. Israel Abrahams. 2 vols. Jerusalem: Magnes, 1961.

Daniélou, Jean. *In the Beginning . . . : Genesis I–III.* Baltimore: Helicon, 1965.

Davidson, Robert. *Genesis 1–11.* The Cambridge Biblical Commentary. Cambridge: At the University Press, 1923.

Driver, Samuel Rolles. *The Book of Genesis.* London: Metheun, 1904.

Dubarle, A.M. *The Biblical Doctrine of Original Sin.* Trans. E.M. Stewart. New York: Herder and Herder, 1964.

de Franine, Jean. *Adam and the Family of Man.* Trans. Daniel Raible. Staten Island, N.Y.: Alba, 1965.

——————. *The Bible and the Origin of Man.* New York: Desclee, 1962.

Grelot, Pierre. *Man and Wife in Scripture.* Trans. Rosaleen Brennan. New York: Herder and Herder, 1964.

Gunkel, Hermann. *The Legends of Genesis: The Biblical Saga and History.* New York: Schocken, 1964.

Haag, Herbert. "The God of the Beginnings and of Today." In *The Unknown God.* Ed. Hans Kung. New York: Sheed and Ward, 1966, pp. 45–90.

——————. *Is Original Sin in Scripture?* Trans. Dorothy Thompson. New York: Sheed and Ward, 1968.

Hauret, Charles. *Beginnings: Genesis and Modern Science.* Trans. E.P. Emmans. Dubuque: Priory Press, 1955.

Kravitz, Nathaniel. *Genesis: A New Interpretation of the First Three Chapters.* New York: Philosophical Library, 1967.

McKenzie, John L. *The Two-Edged Sword: An Interpretation of the Old Testament.* Milwaukee: Bruce, 1956.

Rahner, S.J., Karl. "Evolution and Original Sin." In *The Evolving World and Theology*. Concilium 26. New York: Paulist Press, 1967, pp. 61–73.

Renckens, Henricus. *Israel's Concept of the Beginning*. New York: Herder, 1964.

Robert, A., and Feuillet, A. *Introduction to the Old Testament*. New York: Desclee, 1968.

Sarna, Nahum M. *Understanding Genesis*. New York: McGraw-Hill, 1966.

Schoonenberg, S.J., Piet. *Man and Sin: A Theological View*. Trans. Joseph Donceel, S.J. London: Sheed and Ward, 1965.

Skinner, John. *A Critical and Exegetical Commentary on Genesis.* The International Critical Commentary, 1. New York: Scribner's, 1960.

Smulders, Piet. *The Design of Teilhard de Chardin*. Westminster, Md.: Newman, 1967.

Speiser, E.A. *Genesis*. Anchor Bible, 1. Garden City, N.Y.: Doubleday, 1964.

Tennant, Frederick Robert. *The Sources of the Doctrines of the Fall and Original Sin*. New York: Sch ⌐ken, 1968.

Trooster, S. *Evolution and the Doctrine of Original Sin*. Trans. John A. Ter Haar. New York: Newman, 1968.

Van Der Leeuw, G. *Religion in Essence and Manifestation*. Trans. J.E. Turner. New York: Harper and Row, 1963.

Vawter, Bruce. *A Path through Genesis*. New York: Sheed and Ward, 1956.

von Rad, Gerhard. *Genesis: A Commentary*. Trans. John H. Marks. Old Testament Library. London: SCM, 1961.

1